Autistic pathology

Elie Letourneur

Autistic pathology

An integrative approach to multi-factorial phenomena

ScienciaScripts

Cover image: www.ingimage.com

This book is a translation from the original published under ISBN 978-613-8-42450-5.

Publisher:
Sciencia Scripts
is a trademark of
Dodo Books Indian Ocean Ltd. and OmniScriptum S.R.L publishing group

120 High Road, East Finchley, London, N2 9ED, United Kingdom
Str. Armeneasca 28/1, office 1, Chisinau MD-2012, Republic of Moldova, Europe

ISBN: 978-620-7-30082-2

Acknowledgements

This dissertation was made possible by the contributions of a number of people, to whom we would like to express our gratitude.

We would first like to thank Mr Lucien Hounkpatin for agreeing to supervise this work and for his attentive supervision. We would also like to thank the co-jurors for agreeing to take part in the reading and defence process.

We would like to thank the Association Autisme Espoir Vers l'Ecole, its director and members, for the training they gave us on autism, for their presence, their work and what it brought us in writing this thesis.

We would also like to thank the entire team at the Centre Lud'éveil, both professionals and volunteers, for their many contributions, which helped us to develop this work well beyond our initial ambitions. We are particularly grateful to Pauline Quinat, clinical psychologist, for her trust, openness, encouragement and sound advice. We would also like to thank Aliénor Comier, clinical psychologist, for her availability and for all the conversations that helped inform our thinking. Finally, we would like to thank the children at the centre for the many experiences they allowed us to share with them, for their welcome and, above all, for their smiles. Finally, we would like to say how grateful we are to their parents, who agreed to answer our many questions and engage in lengthy discussions. We would like to offer our sincere support to these families and professionals, so that their work continues, and to express our utmost respect for them.

TABLE OF CONTENTS:

CHAPTER 1

1. Introduction

1.1. Choice of subject

The issue of autism came to the fore as a result of our placement and the questions it raised. For several months, we had the opportunity to carry out comprehensive observations with six autistic children (aged 2.5 to 16) at the Lud'éveil centre in Courbevoie, which is affiliated to the Autisme Espoir Vers l'École (AEVE) association. Through weekly one-and-a-half-hour play sessions with each of the children, we were able to familiarise ourselves with the issue of autism, and set out to explore the range of possibilities that this complex, protean pathology can take on.

In the course of our reflections, we have fluctuated a great deal, we have amended a great deal, and we have been confronted with a succession of doubts and certainties which have benefited us in our understanding of pathology, patients, their problems, and the very particular prism through which they perceive their reality.

We were also able to refine our view of the institutions providing care for autistic patients, and understand the issues at stake, as well as appreciate the realities of their day-to-day operations. This gave us a glimpse of how theoretical presuppositions can influence the way care is provided *in situ*, and conversely how practical realities as experienced by care professionals can in turn profoundly modify the theoretical acceptances to which they relate. We were particularly sensitive to this bi-directionality, which seems to us to be representative of the theoretical and clinical abundance to which autism is subject.

It seemed to us that a number of clichés about this pathology were dangerously entrenched in people's minds, both in the considerations of the general public and in the supposed knowledge of certain professionals dealing with this vast issue. A number of fixed ideas, the result of decades of misguidance and neglect in the field, still seem to be in force today. However, we have observed that many of these presuppositions are not necessarily borne out in practice with autistic children, or at least do not constitute recurrent clinical signs. This is why we have endeavoured to discern the wheat from the chaff in the mass of information that constitutes the basic breeding ground of our societies' knowledge of phenomena relating to autism.

1.2. Writing style

After a difficult period of immersion in the world of autism, mainly due to the theoretical and clinical chaos from which our subject of study suffers, and the difficulty of making contact with patients (or at least understanding their actions), we decided to start from scratch with our conceptual work and our appreciation of the patients in our care. It was in this context of 'intellectual virginity' that we chose to attempt to understand the ins and outs of this pathology. Far be it from us to deny the many contributions made by research and clinical practice, let alone to fail to draw inspiration from them, but we nevertheless wanted to free ourselves from any ideological straitjacket, in order to construct what we hoped would be an intelligent and refined piece of research, taking less account of current theories than of the phenomena observed during the course of the year.

To do this, we will take the time to present the main disorders of autism, review its history, and provide a selected overview of the related literature and existing treatment methods in order to understand the context. Most of our work will then consist of exploring and attempting to embrace as many dimensions of this pathology as possible, with a view to reflecting on those that struck us most in the clinic during our placement, in order to understand, for example, how certain a priori irreconcilable aspects manage to coexist, as well as to shed light on certain phenomena that appear incomprehensible at first glance, in clinical settings where communication so often eludes the practitioner.

More broadly, we wanted to try to understand the issues surrounding autism, in particular by paying as much attention to detail as possible. It was in this way that we found it most relevant to study the sometimes enigmatic behaviour of patients. Without claiming to explain them, we set out to list in minute detail the most minute recurrences or analogies that we witnessed, so that we could discuss them. It seemed to us that it was by observing their actions, without having any preconceived ideas about their importance or uselessness, that we would be able, if not to remove the mystery, at least to understand the wrinkles in their veil.

From then on, the question of semiology, and above all diagnosis, will be a key focus of our work. This is a point that has raised many questions throughout our discussions. The sometimes fine line between autism (as it is currently diagnosed) and other pathologies has led us to look at the question of diagnosis in a different light. We have asked ourselves what motivates a diagnosis on the part of the practitioner, how it is influenced by the context and its agents, what social representations are associated with it, and how much responsibility they may assume in its formulation.

We also wanted to give our work an honest and constructive critical perspective. In doing so, we have sought to explore the limits of modern care, to understand them, and to try to make some observations. Without claiming to have any new truth about autism, what we have sought to do here is to take stock of the theoretical, clinical, practical and institutional aspects. It seemed to us that unravelling this pathology was in itself a valuable contribution, enabling us, as future professionals, to trace its contours and limits and to understand the reasons for it.

The main question we will be asking as we embark on these reflections is that of the multifactorial nature of autism, a cross-disciplinary pathology whose determinants seem to us to be sociological, moral, representational, historical, environmental, clinical, familial and individual.

4

1.3. Methodological point

With regard to the methodology adopted during the observations made at the Lud Eveil centre, we would like to point out that the constraints of the location and the ins and outs of the method promoted considerably complicated matters. In fact, we had to adapt the formal requirements of academic rigour to a rather fluid and undefined context. To do this, we tried to control as many variables as possible, such as the place, the time, our attitude towards the patient, the way in which we wrote up the session reports, and so on. Despite this, the fact remains that the association where we did our placement does not allow us to have the rigour that we would have liked for this university clinical work. However, it seems to us that we managed to limit the most important biases and that we were able to overcome the formal problems we were faced with.

In addition, we have chosen to present autistic pathology in chronological order, in order to reflect the evolution of ideas on the subject. While it is true that this method may seem somewhat linear, we felt that it was well-suited to the issue of autism and provided the overview needed to understand the current ins and outs of this disease. History works here as a logical lens through which to view what is happening today, and it seems to us that it would have been detrimental to deprive ourselves of this diachronic perspective.

2. Autistic pathology

2.1. Definition

To give a concrete definition of autism is in itself a challenge. Understanding and delimiting this pathology is indeed a complex process, since it seems that its clinical forms, manifestations and causes are multiple.

The term allows us to circumscribe the subject *a priori*: derived from the Greek *autoç* meaning self, it seems that one of its primary characteristics is that the subject has a relationship only with himself. Both accurate and erroneous, this assertion nevertheless enables us to understand the state of mind in which the practitioner, but also the general public, may find themselves when faced with a subject presenting this pathology.

More officially, autism, or should we say autistic disorders, is a series of pathologies in which the essential characteristic is a triad of impairments in social interaction, communication and imagination (the latter being illustrated in particular by a series of restricted and repetitive behaviours).

This includes infantile autism (Kanner type), Rett syndrome, atypical autism, Asperger syndrome, hyperactivity associated with mental retardation and stereotyped movements, childhood disintegrative disorders and other unspecified pervasive developmental disorders. These nosographic biases are derived from the DSM-IV and ICD-10, which classify them in the Pervasive Developmental Disorders (PDD) category, as does the CFTMEA, which also refers to early-onset psychoses. It should be noted that since 2013, autism has been included in the category of Autistic Spectrum Disorders (ASD - DSM 5). Developed in 1979 by Judith Gould, a psychologist, and Lorna Wing, a psychiatrist and physicist, the concept of the continuum or autistic spectrum offers the possibility of a more detailed clinical assessment, since each of the elements of the triad and its manifestations can be moderated and quantified in order to better assess the nature and intensity of the disorders and identify the form of pathology we are dealing with.

We can see the extent to which the establishment of a perfect and indisputable definition is out of reach. Indeed, the relationship between the patient and his or her practitioner or even his or her family will be extremely different, depending on whether the patient is closer to an Asperger's or Kanner-type diagnosis. This is why we feel that the modern definition of autistic spectrum disorder is the most appropriate, given the diversity of patient profiles and the needs of care. In practice, we observe that the different aspects of the disease can take on completely different forms and intensities. What's more, certain features can act as a screen for other dimensions, making it more difficult to analyse and understand the subject. For our part, and in order to have a privileged axis on which to base ourselves, we will take the decision to apprehend autism mainly in terms of the following aspects: on the one hand, isolation in the face of otherness and withdrawal into one's own universe, and on the other, the sensory aspects that the pathology reveals. We will also attempt to deal with the question of stereotypies and regression phenomena, since their manifestations seem to us to be fruitful for analysis, despite the perplexity in which they sometimes leave us. We will not confine ourselves to defining autism in terms of its symptoms and related features, but will also seek to understand what this pathology means for the subject himself, in its clinical dimension, and in its relationship to care. In our view, this particular form of pathology, as well as the history of its emergence, makes it necessary to refer to various disciplines, some of them distant, so as not to restrict our understanding of it to an overly narrow field of study, which would only lead us astray. It is also because autistic disorders affect many strata of the subject's life that we have forced ourselves to consider this multidisciplinary approach.

2.2. Logic-historical development

There are many hypotheses to address the persistent shortcomings of the autism clinic. It has been considerably enriched over time by currents of thought that are sometimes opposed but always constructive. In order to fully understand its nature and evolution, we have chosen to place it in a diachronic perspective, by looking back two centuries.

2.2.1 . Early 19th century[ème] : First controversies

At the time, the terminology was different, with the term idiotism or idiocy being used, and different nosographic entities being assimilated, as we distinguish them today. However, the literature mentions cases that can easily be compared to autism as we think of it today.

The famous case of Victor de L'Aveyron is one such example. Captured by hunters in the Aveyron forests on 8 January 1800, he was first taken to the orphanage at Saint Affrique. Constant Saint-Estève, commissioner at Saint-Sernin, was the first to comment on the subject. He assumed he was around twelve years old, and stated that he appeared to be "*deaf and dumb from birth*"[1] . It should be noted that today an ENT examination is often one of the first that is suggested to parents when they think they are dealing with an autistic-type symptomatology, in order to find out whether a real hearing problem can explain the unusual behaviour. After a brief stay with Abbé Bonnaterre, the young boy was transferred to Paris on the orders of the Minister of the Interior.

Philippe Pinel, the famous alienist physician of the time, came to the conclusion that the boy was retarded from birth, that he could not be educated, and went so far as to suggest that this was probably the reason why his parents had abandoned him. Apart from these conclusions, which may seem somewhat brutal, Pinel had the merit of leaving a detailed description of the young man's visible

---

[1] Lane, H. (1979). L'enfant sauvage de l'Aveyron. Paris: Payot.

symptoms. These undoubtedly echo our current understanding of autism: failure to fix one's gaze on an object, fleeting and intermittent attention, no established deafness but only reactions to particular sounds (such as those of food), unintelligible cries, constant rocking, inability to form satisfactory intersubjective relationships, insensitivity to play. Considered incurable, the child would no longer be of interest to Pinel and the doctors in his circle.

On the other hand, Jean Itard, head physician at the institution for deaf mutes in Paris, thought that a suitable teaching method could enable the child to make progress, particularly in acquiring normal sensitivity or learning to speak. He therefore defends the theory of a moral disorder to which treatment can be applied. It is important to remember that philosophers at the time were engaged in heated debates about the notions of the state of nature and culture. The central question was whether ideas were innate or whether they were assimilated during the educational and developmental process. In fact, this question of organic versus psychological origin remains one of the key issues in the debate on autism to this day. Itard's notes include the hypothesis that Victor's disorder (as he renamed it) could be the result of too little human contact in early childhood. Dr Itard envisaged a treatment based on sensory stimulation and learning through repetition and habituation to recognise and distinguish common stimuli. He applied a graduated method using increasingly complex exercises, in order to maintain satisfaction in learning, which also showed that he intended a certain form of affectivity for this young boy. From this point of view, Itard noted that Victor gradually became very attached to his governess and learned to laugh and cry. He also managed to dress himself and sleep in a bed rather than on the floor. However, the Doctor's perseverance and four years of intensive care did not enable him to acquire language. Doctor Itard eventually gave up, and Victor died in total solitude in 1828.

Itard's detractors will say that Victor was less impressive than a trained monkey, but it has to be said that the progress made was not anecdotal and today would constitute a relatively satisfactory stage in the treatment of autism. Victor de l'Aveyron's episode did nothing, however, to change the conditions under which the children of the time, now known as autistic, were cared for. They remained interned in hospitals without any specific care, and did not arouse the interest of professionals.

2.2.2 . Mid-19th century: The Age of the Alienists

It was not until Édouard Séguin that this population was studied again. Having received advice from Itard and then Esquirol on potentially applicable educational methods, and having been put in charge of a class of defective children by Esquirol, on whom he made his first observations, he opened a public school in Paris in 1840, specialising in the care of idiots. This comprehensive care advocated a certain level of material comfort, good hygiene, healthy food and decent clothing. He considered that the immobility of his subjects was problematic and required regular gymnastics and sensory stimulation, which, in his opinion, led to an awareness of the body schema, which these children had

8

difficulty representing and feeling. Séguin also devised the first educational games (matching, stacking, building, sorting), which he saw as "*the forceps of intelligence*"[2] . But he was not a doctor, and came in for fierce criticism from the scientific community. A source of jealousy, he also suffered from numerous administrative difficulties that made his professional life complicated. After the coup d'état of Louis Napoléon Bonaparte (Napoléon III) in 1851, and the restoration of the Empire in 1852, Séguin decided to go into exile in the United States. There, his work was fully appreciated, and he contributed to the opening of numerous institutions and to the development of approaches derived from his own. Séguin's importance is great, as it is true that his method would later return from the United States in the form of various intensive, educational, cognitive or multisensory variations (Doman, TEACCH, ABA). After Séguin's departure and until the end of the 19th century, there were no publications of note concerning idiot children.

2.2.3 . End of the 19th century: First treatments

Some thirty years later, Désiré Magloire Bourneville reused the work of Séguin, whose book entitled Rapports et mémoires sur l'éducation des enfants normaux et anormaux (1895) he prefaced following the Vienna Universal Exhibition. The highlight of his contribution to the clinic for autistic children was the introduction of his adapted class programme in the department for idiot children that he ran at Bicêtre Hospital. He set up a medical-educational programme, run by both a care team (nurses) and a teaching team (teachers) under the supervision of a doctor, whom he himself represented. His approach, which undoubtedly prefigured the way autistic children are treated today, was nevertheless strongly contested at the time. The incurability of this pathology, supported by many professionals at the time, raises the question of the validity of any form of treatment.

2.2.4 Early 20th century^{ème} : Emergence of the term "Autism".

One of the leading figures in this challenge was Dr Alfred Binet, who, after having virulently attacked Séguin in his 1907 book Les Enfants anormaux, challenged Bourneville's considerations, relying on the concept of intelligence quotient, which he invented. According to his logic, below a certain score it is illusory to hope for any intellectual acquisition whatsoever.

At the time, the United States and Protestant Northern Europe were carrying out sterilisations on these populations in order to preserve the quality of the race of normal beings. In 1909, Bourneville died and his programme was stopped, as the cost was deemed too high for subjects who were then once again considered incurable.

It would be wrong to classify Maria Montessori as a practitioner specialising in autism (or its equivalents), but it is worth noting the important role she played in passing on the work of Séguin

---

[2] Séguin, E. (1895). Rapport et mémoires sur l'éducation des enfants normaux et anormaux. Paris: Alcan.

and, more anecdotally, Itard. In this way, she acted as a conduit for certain clinical approaches that have come down to us.

The word autism was first used in 1911. It was Eugène Bleuler who coined the term to describe the nature of the thinking and withdrawal characteristic of the nosographic group of schizophrenias. If chronologies relating to autism often do not cover the years between 1911 and 1943, it is probably because the schizophrenias studied by Bleuler when he coined the term had long encompassed the clinical entity we know today. Long included in the ranks of early-onset dementias, then described in the 1920s as

It is also known as childhood schizoid psychopathy by Grounia Soukhareva, who describes it as a *"questioning attitude"* ([3]). What remained constant throughout these years was the consensus that he had lost touch with reality.

2.2.5 Mid-20th century*ème* : First theories

Melanie Klein

In 1930, Melanie Klein used the term infantile schizophrenia when referring to children suffering from *"stereotypies"*[4] and a *"lack of emotional contact"*[5]. She was one of the first to offer a clinical description of a syndrome now identified as autism. Indeed, in her Dick case, under the heading of infantile psychosis, we see a clinical picture very similar to the disorder we are interested in. She describes him as having *"non-existent affective relationships and being almost totally devoid of affect"*[6], taking no interest in anything, not playing and having no contact with the people around him. Most of the time, Dick simply uttered inane babble. Even more than being unable to communicate, he seemed to have no desire to do so. He showed great insensitivity to pain and had a *"fixed, distant and indifferent expression"*[7]. On the other hand, he showed an obsessive interest in certain objects such as trains or door handles. It is easy to recognise the typical symptoms of autistic syndrome as we know it.

Léo Kanner

In 1943, Leo Kanner, a child psychiatrist of Austro-Hungarian origin who had emigrated to the United States, published his observations on the behaviour of eleven children under his care.

"Since 1938, our attention has been drawn to a number of children whose condition differs so totally

---

[3] Minkowski, E., Targowla, R. (1923). Contribution à l'étude de l'autisme : l'attitude interrogative. *L'Encéphale*, 395.
[4] Klein, M. (1930). The importance of symbol formation in the development of the ego. In Essais de psychanalyse (pp. 263-278). Paris : Gallimard.
[5] Ibid.
[6] Ibid.
[7] Klein, M. (1930). The importance of symbol formation in the development of the ego. In Essais de psychanalyse (pp. 263-278). Paris : Gallimard.

and radically from anything hitherto described that each case deserves, and I hope will receive, detailed consideration of its fascinating peculiarities"[8]. These words constitute the incipit of the first clinical text to describe an infantile syndrome that Kanner would later call early infantile autism. Kanner observed in his patients a high degree of autistic isolation, an obsessive desire to reject any inconsistency in their environment, a major disturbance in emotional contact and extremely rare spontaneous activities. According to him, most of these children have language, but it has no phatic value. His description remains entirely relevant today, and the Donald case, which was Kanner's first, was long used as a diagnostic model for autism. Kanner's approach was to adopt medical rigour in describing the syndrome and listing its symptoms, without, however, predicting its origin. He nevertheless noted the coldness of his patients' mothers and the distance of their fathers from the family unit. Throughout his life, he oscillated between the organic and psycho-affective hypotheses. In the end, however, he came down on the side of an innate cerebral disorder in which environmental factors are entirely anecdotal.

Hans Asperger

An Austro-Hungarian doctor, like Kanner, he decided to remain on the old continent despite the Anschluss. He began working with children in Vienna in 1926, and among his patients were four boys whom the psychiatrist described as showing a lack of empathy, poor interpersonal skills, unidirectional conversation, intense preoccupation with specific subjects and a certain motor clumsiness. He described the cases of these children in a series of texts entitled Die Autischen Psychopathen im Kindesalter (Autistic Psychopathies in Childhood), published in 1944 in the German journal Archiv für Psychiatrie und Nervenkrankheiten. It should be noted, however, that these texts were written in 1943, which makes them even closer to the timeframe of Léo Kanner's research and his seminal article. However, as Asperger's texts were written in German, they remained unknown for several decades. It was only in 1981 that they resurfaced, until Lorna Wing (theorist, with Judith Gould, of the notion of the autistic spectrum) mentioned Asperger's research, raising its profile tenfold. Since then, everyone knows the importance of the work of Asperger's, whose eponymous syndrome is used to designate autistic people who do not have intellectual mental retardation. By way of anecdote, Hans Asperger himself appears to have suffered childhood disorders comparable to those described in his syndrome. In addition to the work he carried out, he also inspired a number of scientists, including Andreas Rett, who was one of his students and was the first to isolate a genetic neurological disease to which he gave his name.

In the years that followed, autism was initially considered to be a rare syndrome, but little by little

---

[8] Kanner, L. (1943). Autistic disturbances of affective contact. In L'autisme infantile. Introduction à la clinique relationnelle selon Kanner, (trans. G. Berquez), (p.217). Paris: PUF.

publications began to appear on this complex pathology and attempts were made to understand its mechanisms and causes.

2.2.6 1960s-1970s: Hegemony of the American School

Margaret Mahler

On the American scene, Margaret Mahler, a paediatrician and psychoanalyst exiled from Hungary, whose work was based on the ideas of Sigmund and Anna Freud, believed that autism was the result of a failure in the normal process of *"separation-individuation"*[9] , and that it constituted a failure to establish a symbiotic relationship with the maternal object, which could be rooted in the child's maternal reticence or powerlessness. As a result of her bias, she sets up therapies based on the mother-child relationship and modes of interaction. It is important to note that she always distinguished between autism and psychosis, which she saw as the result of two different defence mechanisms in response to the mother's attitude.

Bruno Bettelheim

He was also interested in autism. A doctor of philosophy at the University of Vienna and later a psychoanalyst, he emigrated to the United States after being deported to the Dachau and Buchenwald camps. His work on autism is largely oriented towards institutional therapy, which takes the view that while a harmful environment can have a destructive influence on the individual, a favourable environment can also be beneficial. His theory stresses the almost exclusive responsibility of the mother in the development of the disorder, and uses the term *"refrigerator mothers"*[10] , a term first used by Kanner, but amended in 1969. In a series of interviews in 1974, Bettelheim claimed to have cured many autistic children. His therapeutic approach was to distance the child from its mother by placing it in an institution. His expression *"empty fortress"*[11] , which has remained famous ever since, helps us to understand his understanding of these patients. In the 1970s in France, his work led to the creation of the "places to live" of the anti-psychiatry era, whose limitations and excesses no longer need to be demonstrated.

Subsequently, various authors contributed in different ways to the psychoanalytical theory of autism, but always, following Bettelheim's example, by thinking of it from the psychotic angle and emphasising the primordial role of a lack of maternal affectivity.

This idea of maternal responsibility for autism has long persisted, particularly in countries where psychoanalysis is predominant (France, Switzerland, Argentina), despite Kanner's statement at the inaugural conference of the Autism Society of America in 1969: *"Parents, I acquit you"*. For a long

[9] Bergman, A., Malher, M., Pine, F. (1980). The psychological birth of the human being. Paris: Payot.
[10] Kanner, L. (1949). Problems of nosology and psychodynamics in early childhood autism. *Am J Orthopsychiatry*, 19.
[11] Bettelheim, B. (1967). The Empty Fortress. Paris: Gallimard.

time, he regretted having put forward the hypothesis of a cause linked to a lack of maternal affectivity, and he often pointed out that he had gone back on his considerations in a book entitled In Defence of mothers: how to bring up children in spite of the more zealous psychologists (1951).

It was not until the end of 2007 and the report by the CCNE (Comité Consultatif National d'Ethique) on the situation in France of children and adults with autism that the usual views on this condition were revised. This report states that: "*considering the mother to be guilty of her child's disability, severing the child's links with his mother, waiting for the child to express a desire for contact with the therapist when he is panic-stricken by his surroundings, are all ways of measuring the violence of such an attitude, the suffering it may have caused, and the impasse to which this theory may have led*"[12] .

During the period when care for autistic patients in France was extremely patchy, and suffered from a lack of theoretical diversity on the subject, American behaviourism and its experimental advances had also led to a number of operational and therapeutic developments.

Ivar L0vaas

Ivar L-ovaas, a psychologist and professor of psychology of Norwegian origin who emigrated to the United States after the Second World War, adopted the principles of behaviourism to develop a method for treating autistic children in the 1960s. This method, known as Applied Behavioral Analysis or ABA, is an educational approach based on a methodical analysis of behaviour, combined with intensive care with the central aim of integration into society. The main operational lever is the use of reinforcers, which, in the form of personalised rewards, lead to an increase in adapted behaviour and a decrease in maladaptive behaviour. There are many critics of this method, mainly because it is based on the work of Ivan Pavlov and Burrhus Frederic Skinner on animal conditioning. On the other hand, supporters of ABA argue that all forms of education involve a degree of conditioning and that their method has the advantage of adapting this educational component to the particular requirements of the lives of autistic children.

Eric Schopler

Another major contributor to methods for dealing with autism was Eric Schopler, a clinical psychologist of German-Jewish origin who fled to the United States in 1938. Specialising in child psychology and director of the national Child Research programme, in 1972 he developed a programme to train and help autistic children and their families to manage their conditions. This programme, called the Treatment and Education of Autistic and related Communication Handicapped Children (TEACCH), deliberately distanced itself from all psychoanalytic therapeutic models. The

---

[12] Report by the CCNE. (2007). La situation en France des personnes, enfants et adultes, atteintes d'autisme, (102).

innovative aspect of Schopler's method lies in its collaborative dimension. Schopler believes that parents should be fully-fledged partners for professionals. To this end, they are trained in the rudiments of psychology as well as in the TEACCH method itself. The TEACCH programme is often attractive to parents, particularly because it does not blame the mother for the aetiology of autism. The underlying philosophy is that people with autism have different ways of functioning psychologically from our own, but not necessarily inferior. This is why we advocate taking into account and respecting the "culture" of autism. The method itself is structured around three central themes:

- a developmental and integrative approach that considers all aspects of family, social, medical, educational, sensory and motor life. The programmes are tailored to the child and the objectives are determined in proportion to the child's level, abilities and age.
- collaboration between parents and professionals, in which the skills of each are exploited and parents are seen from the outset as the people with the most knowledge about their children. This valuing of the parental role remains the nodal point of TEACCH.
- structured teaching, which offers the subject whose difficulty in spatio-temporal representation can be a vector of powerful anxieties and for whom the programme advocates a strong structuring of daily life which, without leading to immutability, allows easier reference points leading to increased predictability with the aim of reducing the uncertainty and anxiety associated with it. Like the ABA method, reinforcers are also used to create motivation. The TEACCH method is also unquestionably based on American behaviourist research.

Stanley Greenspan

The last method we wish to discuss was developed by Stanley Greenspan, an American psychiatrist, and was first described in 1979 in his book Intelligence and adaptation. His programme, entitled DIR/Floortime (Developmental Individual-differences Relationship-based), is a developmental model based on identifying the individual's strengths and weaknesses and adapting them through play. Recommending intensive and varied care, it is structured around individual sessions of play and stimulation aimed at establishing a relationship with the autistic individual. It requires the creation of an adapted playroom with sensory stimulation elements and duplicate objects to encourage play sharing. The model comprises nine functional and emotional stages representing the desired evolutionary stages of care, through which the individual aims to gain access to a shared world before finally mastering the symbolic and intellectual aspects of life.

2.2.7. Contemporary period: Rereading American approaches

In addition to the ABA and TEACCH methods, which have become increasingly important in the Old World over the last twenty years or so, there are various adaptations of behaviourist and cognitivist precepts whose visibility is uneven. We have chosen to present just one of these, well aware nonetheless that many other American approaches have been reported in France in recent years.

3i method

This method crossed the Atlantic in the mid-2000s and arrived in France in a derivative form known as the 3i method, for Individual, Interactive, Intensive. It combines the intensiveness and playfulness of DIR/Floortime with the basics of the Son-Rise programme developed by Barry Neil and Samahria Lyte Kaufman in the early 1970s.

It takes shape thanks to the regular involvement of volunteers, clinical psychologists and psychology trainees, who accompany and play with the children, in the play centre or at home, for an hour and a half each per week. This large team is necessary to meet the demands of the children's schedules, which include some forty hours of weekly play sessions. In addition, this requires a play space adapted to each child (a room of about ten square metres arranged and furnished according to the child's needs and preferences, with high shelves to encourage the child's demand for support).

This method recommends not over-stimulating the subjects, but making sure to identify their moments of mental availability, in order to capture their attention at the right moment. This is why it considers it necessary for the practitioner to dispense with any presuppositions about the pathology, any value judgements and to relinquish all control when he comes to play with the child, so as to be in total acceptance of what is presented for observation without directing the course of events. In fact, benevolence is the key word in the care given to 3i children, and everything is designed with the child in mind, so that he or she can progress in an environment that is favourable to him or her.

It is therefore by agreeing to join the child in his world, at his level, and with enthusiasm, as a child of his age would do, that contact is facilitated. This is why the method focuses largely on the child's continuous imitation, which we have found, with patience, can lead to real exchanges with autistic children, who are visibly much more interested in others when they are doing things identical to their own. It is only in this way that the carer will be able to maintain contact with the child, and it is in this way that he will be able to divert the initial imitation through play towards learning. These various precautions are designed to give the child time to develop the neo-Piagetian developmental stages (sensory-motor, pre-operational, concrete operations, formal operations), which the 3i method aims to re-establish, since it considers that the autistic child must have acquired and surpassed these stages before being able to individualise himself, and thus claim to be progressively socialised. It is also for this reason that the children are taken out of school during their treatment, and that the primary vocation is precisely to be the pathway to a return to school.

For your information, this method has not yet been approved by the French National Authority for Health and is still in the process of seeking scientific validation.

Our overview of theoretical developments and the different methods of care that autism research has helped to shape is certainly not exhaustive, but we have made a choice based on the operational and institutional visibility that we felt was most realistic.

The methods presented are in fact the most common, but there are many other treatment proposals derived from them, differing to a greater or lesser extent in their nature (behavioural, developmental, psychotherapeutic) and in their intervention programme, which may be global or, conversely, focused on a particular aspect of the pathology. As far as the 3i method is concerned, we have chosen to mention it mainly because it was applied at our training centre, and because we found it very interesting and useful in our approach to the subjects we were following.

2.2.8. Recent advances in neuroscience

Over the last twenty years or so, neuroscientific research into autism has multiplied, and we now have a number of leads which, while admittedly not sufficient to explain the phenomenon in its entirety, have nonetheless contributed to our understanding of this disorder.

The role of certain hormones and other neurotransmitters is being studied in particular, and a number of related dysfunctions have already been identified.

Oxytocin, commonly known as the birth hormone, controls chlorine levels in the brain of the foetus and triggers a collapse in these levels at birth, inhibiting the associated GABA neurons, which are responsible for neuronal maturation, growth and the creation of synapses. The depolarisation of GABA neurons is in turn influenced by the neuronal chlorine content. GABA has an inhibitory or excitatory effect depending on whether the chlorine concentration is low or high. This concentration depends on the age of the neurons. After birth, therefore, GABA neurons become inhibitory, regulating the electrical activity of the nervous system. Through a series of experiments[13] on animals, Prof Ben-Ari observed that by reducing the neuronal chlorine level of young autistic children through the administration of oxytocin, there was a slight but significant reduction in the behaviour typical of the disorder. What's more, by administering oxytocin to pregnant mothers and administering a substance that blocks oxytocin production to another group, we obtained two distinct groups, the second of which showed autistic symptoms. The role of oxytocin is not yet fully understood, but it

---

13 - Ben-Ari, Y, Cherubini, E., Corradetti, R., Gaiarsa, J.-L. (1989). Giant synaptic potentials in immature rat CA3 hippocampal neurons. [Retrieved January 8, 2015 from http://www.ncbi. nlm.nih.gov/pmc/ articles/ PMC1189216/].
- Ben-Ari, Y. (2007). GABA: a primary transmitter for brain construction. [Retrieved January 8, 2015 from http://www.medecinesciences.org/articles/medsci/full_html/2007/09/medsci2007238-9p751/ medsci2007238-9p751.html#InR2].
- Dhossche, D. (2002). Elevated plasma gamma-aminobutyric acid (GABA) levels in autistic youngsters: stimulus for a GABA hypothesis of autism. [Retrieved January 8, 2015 from http://www.ncbi.nlm.nih. gov/ pubmed/12165753].
- Korsia-Meffre, S. (2014). Autism and related disorders: a new study reinforces the brain chlorine trail. [Retrieved January 8, 2015 from http://www.vidal.fr/actualites/13591/ autisme_et_troubles_apparentes_une_ nouvelle_ etude_renforce_la_piste_du_chlore_cerebral/]

remains one of the main avenues of research.

Serotonin and its modes of action are also being extensively studied in autism research. This neurotransmitter is involved at the cerebral level in various functions such as sleep, digestion and thyme regulation. However, this role in the central nervous system is a minority one, and most of its action takes place in the digestive tract, where it acts as an autacoid, a hormone that acts locally. It should be noted that serotonin production in the brain is influenced by the transport of tryptophan, an amino acid contained in certain proteins. This transport is itself dependent on the concentrations of the other major neutral amino acids, which compete to cross the blood-brain barrier. We can therefore assume that food preferences play an important role in serotonin levels. Furthermore, it would not be the gluten or casein content (as is thought to be the case in the diets of autistic children) that would be problematic for digestion, but the concentrations of tryptophan compared with the other amino acids.

Studies show that a third of autistic children have abnormally high levels of serotonin in their blood platelets. This is not a cause of autism, but rather an observation of how it works. However, we would point out that at the level of the central nervous system, serotonin influences the control of aggression, pain perception, sensitivity to light, mood and physical activity. These various points will make sense in our section devoted to the five senses in autism (*3.2. Sensory aspects of the disorder*).

From a functional point of view, researchers at the Université de Montréal, led by Laurent Mottron of the Centre of Excellence in Pervasive Developmental Disorders, have used a meta-analysis to explain autistic hypersensitivity. They found that "the temporal and occipital regions of the autistic brain are activated more than in non-autistic subjects when they are asked to look at shapes, whether faces, objects or words. These regions are traditionally associated with the perception and recognition of objects".

Lastly, the genetic pathway has also been explored, but this remains exceptionally complex, since multiple genes are involved, with a high degree of inter-individual variability. For these reasons, we will not dwell on this issue, as it seems that there is still too little progress to provide a solid foundation.

These various breakthroughs are often linked to very specific processes and never explain all the behaviours observed. What's more, most observations are only true for a given percentage of the autistic population. This makes understanding the disorder and its causes all the more complex, but it seems that research is making progress and that the future will bring many developments in this field.

2.2.9. Conflicts of approach and conflicts of people

To understand the very special place of autistic pathology in the French clinical landscape, we need to understand its history and the players who have shaped it.

For many years, psychoanalysis was the only accessible response to autism, and as no other treatment was available (or at least not publicly), this discipline was the only one to consider the issues surrounding this illness, and to put in place an effort to understand it and make clinical attempts. As we all know, psychoanalysis at the time had a strong bias, that of a gap in maternity, an emotional deficiency stemming from the mother and constituting the entry into pathology. Bruno Bettelheim spoke of the "refrigerator mother", a somewhat indelicate term to describe mothers for whom maternal affectivity is not self-evident, and who are unable to establish a warm bond with their child. Analytical terminology, because it is often misunderstood and misinterpreted by the general public, has also damaged psychoanalysis, at least in its perceived ability to manage autistic pathology. For example, the use of the term "retarded child" has united a number of parents against the analytical schools.

A certain mistrust, even contempt, of psychoanalysis developed on the part of parents (especially mothers) who felt responsible for their child's illness, an idea that was difficult to accept.

Faced with this terminology and these clear-cut prejudices, parents turned their attention to the New World to observe the methods used to treat autism. Some even made the trip, and soon came back with their arms full of ideas, which they tried to apply to their own children. Numerous associations have been set up by groups of parents who, having obtained results with their own children, wanted to share their experience and offer it to other parents. Psychoanalysis, for its part, has expressed reservations about the clinical relevance of these approaches, and above all about the closed nature of care designed by parents for parents. This was all it took to confirm the conflict that already existed between psychoanalysts and parents' groups.

While we can readily admit that these parents' associations have made it possible to renew somewhat the ideological ground for autism care, the fact remains that this system has its limits because of the excessive collusion between patients and their relatives. In our view, this entails a certain number of risks, which we were able to observe during our internship. The main one is the unbridled desire to see a child develop, even where there is none, a desire that is understandable from an emotional point of view but problematic from a clinical point of view. These days, psychoanalysis has been totally sidelined from the autism debate, along with the issue of parental responsibility, which has become taboo. It seems to us that a happy medium would have been beneficial...

2.3 Brief institutional history

One of the points we are keen to address is the institutional dimension and the evolution of legal provisions relating to autism. To this end, we will conclude our logico-historical development with a review of the various official advances concerning this pathology.

Associative and institutional support for autism as a specific disorder really began in 1963 with the creation of the Fédération Française Sésame Autisme (FFSA), the first association of parents, children and adults with autism, in line with the creation of the first specialised establishment for autistic people.

In 1982, the Association pour la Recherche sur l'Autisme et la Prévention des Inadaptations (ARAPI) was founded, with an equal number of parents and professionals. It was initially designed to organise the 1983 International Autism-Europe Congress in Paris.

In 1989, Autisme France was founded, a parents' association whose primary aim is to guarantee the right of autistic people to be diagnosed, to receive care, to attend school and to have their daily lives less affected by the illness. The association supports the behavioural school approach and complies with the recommendations of the World Health Organisation in this area. Early detection and recognition of parents' skills will be the mainstays of their action. The theory of neurobiological and genetic origin is accepted from the outset, as opposed to a psychological aetiopathogenesis. The association is campaigning for a change in terminology, in line with WHO precepts.

In 1995, Simone Weil, Minister for Social Affairs in the Balladur government, signed an inter-ministerial circular recognising autism as a public health priority. One hundred million francs were earmarked for the creation of 630 places in medico-educational institutes or day hospitals to accommodate these newly recognised populations.

In 1996, the Chossy Act amended the Act of 30 June 1975, which now recognises autism as a specific disability. This status has considerable implications, which we will discuss below.

In 2003, the Chossy report, submitted by the same MP, provided an overview of the situation of autistic people in France. It highlighted significant shortcomings in terms of resources and proposals for this population. For the first time, the report introduced the notion of "passive abuse", a subject that had been avoided until then.

In 2004, the Council of Europe condemned France for its poor management of autistic children and adults, despite two decades of debate on the issue.

The same year saw the creation of the Autism Resource Centres, whose remit is to provide information and guidance to people with autism and their families, to screen for and diagnose the condition, to carry out individual assessments leading to the prospect of treatment, to provide information and training for professionals, and to develop a publication centre to communicate on autism and current affairs.

In 2005, the law on equal opportunities had a significant impact on the care of autistic children, enabling many of them to return to school thanks to the introduction of school life assistants.

In 2007, the CCNE for life and health sciences condemned the dramatic state of care for autistic people in France, which in its view was tantamount to mistreatment.

In 2008, an Autism Plan was launched, comprising thirty measures aimed at providing more information about autism, encouraging the training of specialist professionals, increasing the number of reception centres and improving support for patients with autism.

In 2012, the French National Authority for Health (Haute Autorité de la Santé) published a report listing the guidelines and recommended treatments for autism, recommending multidisciplinary and integrative interventions to minimise maladaptation in the target populations.

In 2013, it was announced that a new four-year Autism Plan would be put in place to implement the HAS recommendations.

Theoretical, institutional and therapeutic developments are mainly moving in the direction of care that enables autistic people to become autonomous rather than being institutionalised. Today, autism has become an illness for which there are places and professionals to turn to. Practitioners are increasingly aware of developments in research in the field, and of institutional responses which, although still incomplete, are becoming more numerous and adapted. Communication has also evolved considerably, benefiting from the explosion in digital resources for disseminating knowledge about the disease.

More recently, following an INSERM report, the French National Authority for Health (HAS) decided to validate the ABA behavioural method as the only institutional treatment for autism. The consequence of this decision is to limit the range of approaches needed to understand a condition that is still poorly understood. Indeed, by limiting the treatment of autism to a single approach, there is a risk that many discoveries that could have been made empirically or through research will be overlooked (since it can be assumed that university grants will be all the more difficult to obtain if they concern research linked to an approach other than the behaviourist ABA method).

3. Clinical observations

In order to be as close as possible to the reality of autism, we chose to dispense with any theoretical presuppositions when assessing the children we followed during our placement. In this way, we were able to naturally extract from our observations what seemed to us to be the most salient, what challenged us the most in the clinic but also in practice, or even what questioned us the most. It is these points that we will discuss, and to which we will attempt to bring some criticism through the presentation of our cases.

3.0 Developmental aspects and archaic issues

3.0.1 Development of the psychic life, structuring of the body schema

The psyche is first established in the body, and it is this body that we need to understand in order to design the organisation of psychic life. The feeling of existing as a subject originates in physical perceptions, in connection with others, in a process that begins in neonatal life.

The work of Esther Bick, as well as that of Donald Woods Winnicott, has shed considerable light on our understanding of this bond, thanks to the meticulous observation of infants and young children.

In utero, the baby is in a warm container that surrounds it, in a permanent sound environment (heartbeat, breathing, digestive noises). The uterine cavity supports the baby's back and head. This first impression is made on the whole of the baby's body, on the back, which creates a hard sensation, but also on the stomach, in a hollow, enveloped by the amniotic fluid, which creates a soft sensation. The first exchanges take place as early as the 4th month, with the baby moving around in the uterus when the mother is at rest.

Gradually, if conditions are good enough, an exchange takes place, in an initial mother-child interaction, as described in haptonomy techniques, with the mother calling her baby by applying gentle pressure to her stomach, and the baby coming to meet the hand that is calling him. This alternating exchange takes place at a time when the child is totally merged with the mother, in a sensation of bi-dimensionality, all on the surface.

At the moment of birth, the mother separates herself from the object she carried within her. The baby is expelled into another container which is still the mother, her arms, her breast, so it remains in continuity with what it experienced in utero.

But if for the mother there is indeed an experience of separation, for the baby this is not the case: "between life in the womb and early childhood, there is much more continuity than the impressive caesura of birth suggests".[14]

---

[14] S. Freud, Inhibition, Symptom, Anguish, Paris, PUF, 1951, p 63

The infant remains attached to the mother, and this bonding sensation continues in the mouth-nipple experience, which brings the child and mother together in an inseparable way, in a container-content relationship. At this stage, the mouth-nipple object is experienced as a containing skin, which Frances Tustin describes as an "adhesive equation", a prerequisite for "adhesive identification".[15]

When Winnicott said, "There is no such thing as a baby"[16] , he was sticking as close as possible to concrete, everyday reality, and in so doing he demonstrated the impossibility of accurately describing the infant's primary affective development without reference to the environment. Indeed, no baby can survive without the active gaze directed at him. So the starting point is not the baby, but the "infant-nurse couple" referred to by Winnicott. This "living creature, surrounded by space" is thus contained within the mother without knowing that space is maintained by the mother. When he moves part of his body (shoulder, knee), "space is crossed". When, "carried by the mother, she is startled by a foreign noise, he experiences himself as existing in an environment that surprises him".[17]

In a sufficiently good environment, where it feels supported, the baby's gaze will turn to the mother. From being a baby who is looked at by the mother, he or she will become a baby who looks, then a baby who asks for the breast and, at the same time, the mother's desire to give him or her the breast. The first ex utero interactive exchanges take place.

In his description of the drive circuit, Freud (1972) defines three stages:

First, the baby is active, moving towards the object of satisfaction, the breast, and then, in an autoerotic relationship, takes its body as the object of satisfaction.

The third stage of the impulse, which Marie-Christine Laznik focuses on in particular, is the one that completes the impulse circuit. The baby offers a part of its body for its mother to "taste" if it is good; then the mother plays at pretending to taste: "you could eat baby like that! Finally, the baby shows his joy at having aroused the pleasure that he reads on his mother's face (scopic drive) and in her voice (invocative drive).

The primary processes, prior to any possibility of representation, are therefore processes of sensations of pleasure and displeasure, more primitive than perceptions, and therefore prior to any consciousness that might lead to the constitution of the ego.

Sensations are at the origin of psychological development, and the way in which they are experienced by newborn babies affects their entire psychological development. Thus, from the experience of a baby-mother object, the child enters the experience of a separation which is at the same time a continuity, the breast becoming the child's containing envelope. The feeling of existing as a container-content enables the child to structure its bodily organisation and experience itself as a unified body.

---

[15] F. Tustin, Les états autistiques chez l'enfant, Paris, Seuil, 2003, p 72
[16] D. W. Winnicott, L'enfant et le monde extérieur, Paris, Payot, P.B. P., 1975, p 107
[17] D. W. Winnicott, Le bébé et sa mère, Paris, Payot, 1987, p 38

For this to become part of the child's psyche, sensations must be transformed into perceptions by another, who serves as a receptacle and reflects the perception, transforming it into a representation. The "mirror-mother" (Winnicott) thus lends her "thinking apparatus" (Bion) to the infant by putting words full of meaning on what she perceives from her many sensations.

As Bernard Golse (1999) describes it, the baby is initially subject to chaotic excesses of excitation, which cannot be metabolised unless filtered by the baby and the parent. There is a need for interactive guidance in order to find one's bearings and gain access to ambivalence, rather than just the juxtaposition of sensations. The mother, who acts as an excitation barrier for the baby, transforms the baby's sensations by providing feedback that is modified by her gaze, and it is this process that establishes a mother-baby/baby-mother agreement, the premise of the first intersubjective relationships.

This time of attunement enables children to unify their sensations and construct a body schema that will give them the feeling of existing as a complete and unfragmented being. It is "the support on the body of the other which allows, by the play of synchronies and exchanges, a progressive detachment of the space of fusion created by the tonic dialogue".[18]

3.0.1 What is not at play in autism

How can autistic children feel they exist thanks to the gaze of another when the radical disorder of autism lies in the impossibility of feeling they are a subject and of establishing a link between a self and a non-self?

This question, which is particularly crucial in autism, takes us back to the way in which their body schema has or has not been constructed. The various behavioural manifestations (tonus disorders, hypotonia or hyperkinesia, synchronisation difficulties, bizarre posture, borrowed gait, psychomotor clumsiness, stereotyped movements, hyper/hyposensitivity, gaze peculiarities, etc.) reveal a profound disturbance in the construction of the body schema, the perception of the body image, and consequently, the feeling of existing.

If the sensory register on which bodily experience is built becomes the containing envelope for psychic content, thoughts must rely on the double support of the skin referred to by D. Anzieu in Le Moi-peau (1985), the skin as the body's surface and the environment as the child's external support. If the body envelope is unable to play its role as a container for thoughts, it is the psychic life that is at stake, and this is what we observe with autistic children who seem so devoid of thought.

To understand what is lacking in the autistic child, undermining the possible relationship with a non-ego and an ego, we need to go back to the body and the organisation of its construction.

---

[18] A. Bullinger, "Approche instrumentale de l'autisme infantile", Le développement sensori- moteur de l'enfant et ses avatars, Toulouse, Erès, 2005, p 151

We feel it is important to quote the words of Fabien Joly, doctor in psychopathology and coordinator of the Bourgogne C.R.A., when he spoke at the 2013 Forum of the A.E.V.E. association. This is confirmed by the testimony of an autistic woman, Steph, who talks about the focus on the autistic triad (communication, language and social interaction disorders), whereas the hidden face of the iceberg is the functioning of the autistic child's body.

However, as M.C. Laznik describes, in autistic children, the third stage of the drive is lacking, and this generates a kind of "stupefaction" at the moment of awareness of the separation of nipple and mouth, a feeling that is closer to a tearing away than to a separation. Without feeling that the mother can absorb and digest her multiple sensations, in the form of a "maternal reverie" (Bion, 1979), and restore them to her in an assimilable way, the baby is frozen in a state of hyper-sensoriality with no container. This triggers a primitive anxiety that stems from a feeling of major risk of non-existence.

The baby has no unity and no sense of continuity of bodily existence. The experience of separation from the mother occurred suddenly and too early, when the child was not ready to feel, with its rudimentary psychic apparatus, the sensory excitations to which it had been exposed, and it did not find a container good enough to experience a separation that was not a wrenching.

We are wondering about the strength of this experience of 'possible non-separation' that manifests itself in autism, whether at the early infant stage, or in secondary autism, when after a development that seemed normal, the child regresses to the point of finding himself at a primitive stage where his own body still has no real existence for him.

Our aim here is not to explore the causes, but to explore the bodily experiences of autistic children in order to understand how therapeutic treatments for autism do or do not enable a bodily 'remodelling' that gives access to an intersubjectivity in which there is an 'I' and an 'other'.

For the autistic child, therefore, there is an experience of traumatic rupture linked to a kind of premature psychic birth, when the experience of primary fusion had not reached the stage of constitution of an ego capable of tolerating its separation from the object.

Frozen at the stage of sensory inscriptions, they are forced, as a survival reflex, to separate their multiple sensations so as not to be overwhelmed by them. This produces the particular image of the body of autistic children, a dismantled body, as described by Donald Meltzer (1980), with separate perceptual capacities - seeing, touching, hearing, smelling - reducing the object to a multiplicity of uni-sensory events in which animate and inanimate become indistinct, where sensations are juxtaposed, unconnected to one another. The child is in a situation of sensory saturation.

Daniel N. Stern has particularly described this lack of 'transmodality' in autistic children, whose five senses (which Alain Berthoz supplements with two other senses: proprioception and the sense of balance) cannot be 'switched on' at the same time. The response, usually provided by the mother to the child through a communication channel other than the one used by the child, cannot be heard.

There is no mutatis mutandis communication that allows sensory correspondences, because the functioning of the autistic child is in a way "single-take" and not "multi-take".

However, Suzanne Maiello's theory highlights an experience of continuity and discontinuity from the original state in utero. During foetal life, there seem to be proto-experiences of separation through what is played out with the sound object[19] . Fetal auditory development is complete around 4ème months, at which point the baby can distinguish between medium- and high-frequency sounds (the mother's voice) and low-frequency sounds (heartbeat, breathing, digestive sounds). These first acoustic perceptions can be distinguished by their continuity or discontinuity. The internal sounds are repetitive and rhythmic, whereas the external mother's voice is discontinuous, unpredictable and uncontrollable. It stimulates the foetus, while low-frequency sounds soothe it.

S. Maiello therefore hypothesises early interaction and vocal and auditory communication between mother and baby, which presupposes a small space of separation. It seems that the autistic child's experience of impossible separation is nonetheless based on archaic experiences of alternating continuity and discontinuity, which are not distressing because they are contained in the womb. Was it at birth, then, that something upset the fragile balance of these proto-experiences of separation?

Shattered by the explosion of their sensations, terrified by the "black hole" that threatens to engulf them, as described by F. Tustin (1989), autistic children cleave, separate and annihilate all affect, collapsing or stiffening in a desperate search for a sense of existence. As Chantal Lheureux-Davidse describes it, "when the autistic child becomes clipped in his bodily sensations, he temporarily leaves psyche and soma to take refuge in his thoughts (...). In this way, the child's sensoriality becomes fragmented and each sense becomes independent of the others, no longer finding a link with the other senses".[20]

It is therefore the sensory-motor functioning that makes it possible to understand autistic functioning. The mass of information to be processed, with this non-globalising perception, accumulating all the details, described by T. Grandin, becomes a real brake on any interaction. It is not so much the intensity of perceptions as their number and frequency that gives this curious impression of "extreme slowness of sensory integration" described by C. Lheureux-Davidse (Cerisy-2014 conference), which puts them out of step in any relationship with another. This is not a desire to ignore the other: they act with a delay that is necessary for them to first settle at the level of their perceptions.

3.1. Otherness in autism

The question of otherness has always been one of the central notions in practitioners' and theorists'

---

[19] S. Maiello, " Trames sonores et rythmiques primordiales ", in Journal de Psychanalyse de l'enfant n° 26, Paris, Bayard éditions, June 2000, pp 77-104

[20] C. Lheureux-Davidse, " Jouer avec les mouvements, les vibrations et les rythmes de l'émergence de la voix ", in Champs Psy, 2007, n° 48, Ed Esprit du temps p 185

assessments of the disorder we now call autism, because of the difficulties in intersubjective relationships that are observed in these patients. Several concepts resonate within this vast question: communication, language, interaction, relationship, investment. All these notions deserve to be rethought and approached from a different angle when studying autism. For a long time, and perhaps still today, some people maintain that autistic patients are incapable of any kind of relationship with others. We believe that this assertion needs to be tempered, and that it is possible that these subjects have a way of apprehending reality that is so radically different from that of most people that their relational modalities are marked by an opacity that borders on incomprehension and, unfortunately, rejection.

We will therefore question both the common presuppositions concerning the relational aspects of autism and the clinical manifestations we have observed.

3.1.1. Language issues and relationships with others

When dealing with an autistic person, it is necessary to rethink the question of relationships. Language is one of the main vectors of relationship, since it enables symbolisation, communication and exchange between two or more partners.

With so-called verbal autistic people, those who have language and agree to use it, it is possible to establish effective communication. Thanks to language, a certain number of interactions are made possible. However, the way in which autistic people, even those who are verbal, approach relationships is very different. It seems that it is in the sphere of relationships that they experience the most difficulties on a daily basis. It should also be noted that these relational difficulties vary greatly from one individual to another, as well as within individuals, depending on the person and the context. We can see that language alone cannot bring a relationship into being, let alone maintain it.

In the case of non-verbal autistic people, the absence of language is *a* major obstacle. Deprived of this medium, we had to take account of an infinite number of signs and details, the analysis and understanding of which nevertheless enabled us to envisage a certain form of relationship. We use the term "relationship" deliberately. We believe that the relationship is established by recognising the individuality of the other person and taking them into account, rather than by language and communication per se. Indeed, when we came into contact with the non-verbal autistic people we worked with during our placement, we gradually saw links being forged and a genuine relationship being established between them and us, but also between them and other carers. This is why we believe that the relationship is not based solely on these aspects, and are deliberately excluding the question of communication from our development, which is an even thornier issue in autism.

However, it is interesting to note that some treatment methods, such as the Picture Exchange Communication System, use visual exchange systems to enable communication between patients and those around them: by exchanging images or colour coding, the patient is to some extent enabled to express himself. This is a proposal worth considering, since learning to communicate, as a co-production enabling exchange and symbolisation, is also extremely difficult to achieve without some form of language.

Despite these difficulties, we wanted to report some clinical elements of our observation which led us to believe that the relationship did indeed exist with autistic people. Starting from the principle that the most insignificant detail could differ from our understanding and have an impact on the relationship, we were able to isolate various phenomena that led us to this hypothesis. In this context, we will present one of the patients cared for in the facility where we did our placement.

3.1.2. The clinical case of Éléonore

Éléonore is 7 years old and is a little girl with blond pigtails and blue eyes who looks extremely slight. She has been at the centre for 2 and a half years now. She has an autistic syndrome with a variety of characteristics. At first glance, her attitude gives the impression of indifference to the people and world around her. Although she does not speak, she does emit a number of sounds accompanied by breaths of varying intensity. Her sounds are based on the phonemes of the French language, with the addition of certain guttural and dorsal-velar sounds. She sometimes sporadically repeats snatches of songs, two or three words, accompanied by the melody. Some of her voicings sometimes take on a repetitive and confining dimension. Éléonore's stereotypies are relatively few and consist mainly of digital movements and frantic rocking. Éléonore has a number of obsessions with objects such as books, letters and numbers, which have a strong contemplative dimension. She showed that she nevertheless had a certain understanding of them	She shows great interest in activities that involve vestibular and proprioceptive stimulation, such as jumping, climbing, spinning and swinging. She sometimes takes a disproportionate interest in certain details of her environment, especially new objects, which attract her attention and all her energy, but only briefly. She is a very energetic little girl, who can sometimes be extremely laughing and cheerful, or on the contrary, very moody. Certain anxieties can also be identified, particularly in the way they are expressed, such as screaming, crying, withdrawing into the foetal position, seeking physical contact or using stereotypies that reorganise (or at least seem to have a stabilising effect). Resolutely autonomous in her actions, she is somewhat authoritarian when it comes to making others understand, mainly through gestures, what she wants them to do. Lastly, she takes great care to maintain a certain immutability in her daily life and seems very sensitive to changes imposed on

by lining up the letters of the alphabet in the right order and showing us that she knew how to use a clock. She eats very little and accepts virtually only familiar foods. Her diet, set up by her parents, consists of gluten-free, casein-free products with a minimum of fast sugars. She also suffers from regular intestinal problems.	her that require her to re-establish her bearings. It's difficult to know exactly what constitutes a reference point for this child, but we were able to notice that certain minute details could constitute crucial points in the surrounding situation in her eyes.

Of all our patients, Éléonore's symptomatology is the closest to the clinical standards for autism. The follow-up we carried out with this child enabled us to nuance and perfect our understanding of autistic phenomena as we had been able to approach them, particularly through the literature.

To give an example, Michel S. Lévy, a psychiatrist and psychoanalyst, believes that the way in which autistic people relate to others is influenced by the "*cataclysm*"[21] that it represents for the subject. Taking his cue from Francès Tustin, he explains that the usual media of communication, such as voice, words and looks, are perceived as aggression and inevitably provoke suffering and anxiety. In order to protect itself against these daily threats, the subject's psyche would refuse any investment in the other. This investment is *ipso facto* directed towards the ego, which according to Lévy is the only object of investment in the lives of these patients.

3.1.3. Investment and relationship

When you're in contact with human beings, and you're brought into regular contact with them over a given period of time, there are a certain number of things, intuitions, feelings, even sentiments, which, while difficult to explain or demonstrate, are not without interest and accuracy.

Over the months that we followed Éléonore, we noticed that there was undoubtedly an evolution in the relationship we had with her. As with any child, there was initially a period during which we got used to each other and got to know and recognise each other. For a while, this patient was very shy, withdrawing into stereotyped behaviours that often took up most of the session, as if her aim was to avoid seeing us. Eventually it became possible to have a closer relationship with her, and she began to take our presence into account and act accordingly. Éléonore, who was rather solitary in her play at the beginning of the year, increasingly asked us to take part in hers, and joined us with obvious pleasure in our own imitations and activities. She seemed to be gradually relaxing, and the glances in our direction became more and more numerous, more and more fixed, more and more intense.

---

[21] Lévy, M. S. (undated). Autism. [Retrieved March 11, 2015 from http://www.inventionpsychanalyse. com/ autisme.php].

In fact, this was one of the points that struck us most during our placement: although autistic people are said to have an inability to fix their gaze, we were able to observe with all the children at the centre that this difficulty diminished as our encounters progressed. Although we in no way deny that autistic people do avoid eye contact, and that even when they do not, there are difficulties in maintaining eye contact with another person, we are quite certain that this does exist and is sincerely intended. Even if it is difficult to demonstrate these statements other than by experience, there have been many phenomena that have confirmed us in this direction. For example, there were many moments when Éléonore's gaze was clearly sought, as well as that of the other children, who would stand facing us, their foreheads pressed against ours, and could stay like that for many minutes, smiling at us or exploring our faces with their hands. Also, during imitation games, we noticed on several occasions that Éléonore, who was doing acrobatics with her back to us, would turn around to "check" whether our imitation was appropriate.

While it is true that with her the moments involving a form of non-verbal communication are often marked by authoritarianism and the instrumentalisation of our person, this does not seem to us to deprive them of interest. The authoritarian use of others to obtain a desired object or activity is itself a form of omnipotence. However, it seemed to us that this was, in fact, a use of the other that was, at the very least, proof that he or she was being taken into account. When we use someone, we inevitably recognise their usefulness as well as our own needs. In our view, this dynamic is an avenue to be explored in the context of the autism clinic, which should be used in a different way to create relationships and exchanges more suited to human society.

From the point of view of the investment of the other, it seems to us that Michel S. Lévy's assertions should at least be moderated. Lévy's assertions need at the very least to be moderated. If, like him, we assume that this lack of hetero-investment is rooted in the perception of the other as hostile and "*catastrophic*"[22] , then how can we explain the search for comfort that we observed in our young patient, who openly demanded cuddles and caresses when she was unwell? What's more, on several occasions we were greeted by Éléonore with big smiles and songs that we had sung together, and that she never sang with anyone else. On the one hand, this implies that the subject has mentally linked the song and the person, and therefore that a form of recognition exists, but it is also clear that the shared pleasure of singing came back to the young girl's mind when she saw us. This observation leads us to believe that a certain affectivity can exist, even with people who have not always shared their lives, and that autistic children can (in their own particular way) invest in others by taking account of their individuality. Thanks to the monthly information meetings attended by most of Éléonore's carers, we realised that she associated certain activities with this or that person. For

---

[22] Lévy, M. S. (undated). Autism. [Retrieved March 11, 2015 from http://www.inventionpsychanalyse.com/autisme.php].

example, she very regularly wanted us to play with play dough while no one else at the meeting was even aware of its existence. This shows us that the young girl was capable first of recognising us and then of investing in us emotionally, within the framework of our own individuality. It seems to us that denying these aspects of the autistic personality is highly damaging from a clinical and institutional point of view. It would therefore be appropriate to reconsider certain theoretical postulates on which care professionals base themselves, to enable autistic people to be appreciated in a more realistic way.

3.1.4. Self-investment

While Michel S. Lévy maintains that investment in autism is entirely directed towards the ego, which is moreover consistent with his theses that include autism in the group of psychoses and bring it closer to melancholia, we believe that autistic patients could, on the contrary, present a lack of investment in themselves.

One of the first arguments that caught our attention was the absence of pain perception in most subjects. While the contributions of the life sciences have shown that physiological anomalies can exist, we believe that there is something more than a sensory perception defect. If everything could be traced back to this physiological cause, we would simply observe an abnormal reactivity to pain in autistic subjects. However, we have found that it is wrong to say that they do not feel pain. We readily admit that mild pain often provokes no reaction. On the other hand, in the face of more severe pain, we have observed startle reactions, sometimes accompanied by a brief cry and looks or gestures directed at the site of the shock. So it seems that the pain is perceived, but what really seemed to be lacking was the ability to manage it *afterwards*. Their own reaction sometimes even seemed to surprise them, and we observed a certain disarray and a period of indecision and uncertainty following this type of pain. In our view, this is a sign of a lack of ego investment rather than an excess of it. Autistic patients lack the reflexivity and finesse in understanding and perceiving their schema and bodily limits to be able to do something with the nociceptive information that reaches their consciousness.

Furthermore, the difficulties these patients have in understanding and adopting behaviours that are generally accepted by everyone could be explained by this lack of narcissistic investment, leading to a lack of understanding of the social codes of desirability. It also seems that to achieve this level of awareness, it is necessary to be 'clear' about the basis of one's own individuality.

In our view, stereotypies can also be thought of from this angle. The inability to self-involve would leave a certain emotional charge unattached, generating considerable anxiety. Stereotypies then act as an outlet to limit the suffering associated with this difficulty. In this way, they represent a way of expressing an investment that is unable to attach itself to the ego, acting as an outlet. When we reason in this way, we understand the importance of involving otherness with autistic people, if only to allow investment in the other and to come closer to a normal process of emotional management. Ideally, of course, the individual should first learn to invest in the other and then apply the same process to himself.

It should also be noted that it appeared to us that the desire for immutability and the need for reference points demonstrated by autistic people could exist in order to counterbalance a kind of instability of the ego, an inability to consider the permanence of the ego which is projected onto the outside world.

3.1.5. Theories of mind in autism

When we talk about autism, it is generally accepted that this pathology induces a certain deficit in what is commonly known as theories of mind. This ability, which children aged between three and five acquire during normal cognitive development, consists of the child recognising himself and the other person's mental states. This enables them to conceive of differences in points of view, to understand causal links in their environment, and gives them the ability to make inferences about the moods and intentions of others in order to put in place appropriate adaptive strategies. Central to the establishment of rules and therefore to the management of reality, this ability is the necessary premise for a peaceful confrontation with the world.

While it is true that it is difficult to deny that autistic people present a certain number of difficulties in deciphering expressions, it seems to us unjustified to assert that they are totally incapable of mobilising the inferences necessary for theories of mind. As an example, we will refer to three clinical situations which struck us as running counter to these presuppositions.

During a session in which we had taught Éléonore to use tubes of glitter glue, she played on her own for a long time, drawing shapes in different colours. We did the same, sitting opposite her. At one point in the session, we set aside our own sheet of paper and, standing opposite the child drawing on the floor, congratulated her on her achievement. She then raised her head, looked down at her drawing and, looking into our eyes, turned it towards us so that we could see it as it had been produced. This apparently simple gesture nevertheless proves that the young girl is capable of understanding that our point of view differs from hers and that it is necessary to modify the situation so that we can perceive it as she did when she produced it.

The second situation that caught our attention was actually a succession of observations throughout the course. On six or seven occasions, we brought a small bottle of water with us to the sessions for our own consumption. At these sessions, as at all the others, we took Éléonore to the toilet for safety's sake, because it's difficult to know when she wants to go and because she sometimes forgets. On these occasions, and only on the occasions when she had seen us drinking from our little bottle, she tried to get us to sit on the toilet by pulling on our arms and proceeded to undress us. This second example

31

seems to us to illustrate how the subject takes into account the condition of others. It also reveals the linking of distinct situational elements leading to a relevant inference. In this way, we can say that this young patient is capable of a certain number of mental operations that many specialists do not attribute to her.

Our last example leaves more room for interpretation. We cannot state categorically that the phenomenon we observed was not the result of chance. In the association where we carried out our placement, four volunteers working with Éléonore are in fact two couples. In each room there is a visual schedule on which the time slots are filled in with photos of the carers attached with Velcro, and therefore removable. Éléonore regularly manipulates the items on the board and organises their distribution. The schedule is one of the obsessive things she needs to control. On several occasions, she matched the photos of the two couples. However, no one had formally told her that these people were together, and it took a great deal of observation on her part to realise that they were a couple, simply by passing them sporadically. In one of the two cases, she had isolated the photos of the man and the woman and put them on the floor next to each other, refusing to allow them to be put back or exchanged with others for several weeks. Finally, she put them back on the board side by side, in defiance of the logical reality of the schedule, which she usually insists on scrupulously respecting. In the second case, she directly removed the man's photo from its slot and stuck it next to his wife's, where there was a vacant slot and therefore a free space. Each time one of the counsellors from the couple in question joined her in the session, he would take down his photograph and stick it on the board of the counsellor present for the session. Éléonore, who was used to this type of procedure and never showed any reluctance, would take the photo in question each time and make a long series of moves: she would then replace the photo with that of the other spouse, and interchange them by sticking them with Velcro on the board for several minutes, before replacing them side by side on the visual schedule where all the counsellors were. She categorically refused to allow the two spouses to be separated, on two separate boards, and rebuffed anyone who tried to dissuade her, as if in a fit of irritation. We would like to stress that the slightest change made by a third party to the photographs of these two couples would generate an unprecedented outburst, and a series of compulsive behaviours that are totally absent with other photographs. If this pairing is indeed the result of observation and a hypothetico-deductive process on the part of Éléonore, then it would show a finesse in the attributions that leads us to re-evaluate our considerations about autism and their understanding of reality.

These different observations have enabled us to understand, through the case of Éléonore but also other patients, that the theoretical notions linked to autism sometimes suffer from being too radical. While in no way denying their contribution and interest, we believe that it is detrimental to limit too much the capacities that we assume they have. The first works by non-verbal autistic people, made possible by technological advances, allow us to conceive the complexity of the psyche of these patients, and we are only just beginning to glimpse its modalities. The relationship with others is one of the nodal points of the autistic problem. This remains an undeniable fact. However, in our opinion, it is necessary to look beyond the hypothesis of a refusal to communicate, and not stop at the idea of perceiving the other as a terrifying aggression, so as not to limit our understanding and get as close as possible to these patients. Thinking of the psyche of autistic people as merely deficient has the disadvantage of considerably limiting the field of possibilities from a relational and clinical point of view. We believe that if otherness takes on a certain strangeness for these subjects, it is important to understand the reasons for this and to discover ways of adapting to it, as a result of which we may achieve a better understanding of autism and its mechanisms.

3.2. Sensory aspects of the disease

Autism - and this is now a certainty, thanks both to advances in science and to the biographical accounts of patients themselves - is a pathology in which significant sensory disorders can be observed, with multiple variations and variable content. One patient may be hyper-sensitive to a given sense, while another may be hypo-sensitive. There are also variations within the same subject, who may show low sensitivity to one sense and high sensitivity to another, or even over time, as sensory valences may be reversed in the course of a single day.

There have also been reports of synaesthesia, a phenomenon in which the subject perceives an odour as a colour and makes a lasting association between them, only to end up representing the odour in terms of the colour perceived. It even seems that this particular modality of perception is widely experienced by people with autism, which may shed light on the diversity of subjective experiences of the same environment.

We therefore wanted to give a detailed account of the phenomena that we were able to observe during our placement with autistic patients, in order to understand how these specific features could have an importance in the patient's daily life and how it was necessary to consider them in the context of care. With this in mind, we will present the case of Léa, one of our young patients during our placement. We chose to present this case here because it gradually became apparent to us that the sensory aspects of this young patient's inner life were at the root of many observable behaviours and could provide us with a great deal of insight.

The various clinical cases presented below all benefited from the same observation framework, i.e. individual sessions at the Lud'éveil centre, or inter-sessions if necessary. The sessions all lasted 55 minutes and were therefore based on playful interaction with the child. As we have already explained, the methodology here was greatly affected by the constraints of the observation framework. In fact, the only way we had of setting up our observations was to do so within these sessions, despite the limitations and biases that this implies, of which we are aware.

Nevertheless, we have tried as far as possible to make the observation conditions similar so as to obtain coherent reasoning and clinically comparable situations. In short, despite a fluctuating and unusual framework, we wanted to bring as much methodological rigour as possible.

3.2.1. Léa's clinical case

Léa is a young Mediterranean girl who suffers from a form of non-verbal autism, with stereotyped arm movements and obsessive searches for vestibular stimulation, accompanied by phases of apathy and loss of tone which give the observer a feeling of sadness. Not necessarily shying away from contact with others, she solicits them with the intention of obtaining their help in carrying out a planned behaviour. Aware of the need to use others to achieve their ends, they do not go beyond primary authoritarianism, nor do they show the slightest recognition. What's more, the other person's attempts at independence are seen as inadmissible, and there's no question of anyone doing anything on their own in their presence.

On the other hand, she responds very well to imitation, and it's quite feasible to get some degree of cooperation from Léa. What's more, she sometimes imitates the other person, proving that she takes notice and is capable of reproducing things she's heard many times, such as words spoken by her parents in Kabyle.

Léa is naturally quite calm and rather hypotonic. She has an arched posture, is somewhat overweight, and has a swaying gait movements are insecure. Often a little off, she looks around without focusing on anything specific. When she meets someone new, she often greets them by clapping her hands, while encouraging, if not demanding, that the other person do the same. During these moments, she has no difficulty in fixing her gaze and sometimes shares her amusement with the flash of a smile. She is also capable of more outspoken laughter, and of a certain humour that needs to be identified in order to be exploited. Sensory games are the best way to enjoy a pleasant session with Léa. She has a hammock in her playroom and swings in it frantically, undeniably enjoying the stimulation it gives her. This rhythmic compulsion is sometimes useful for getting her out of a state of sensory or emotional overload (can one go without the other?). However, this practice can also take up so much space and time that it renders any presence sterile.

Léa sometimes has moments of great distress, during which she screams and cries, sometimes hitting herself or hard surfaces. These phases are characterised by total opposition to any otherness, which manifests itself in physical violence intended to repel (rather than aggress).

34

whose	

3.1.1. Hearing

Hearing difficulties or abnormalities are often the first signs that lead parents of as yet undiagnosed autistic children to consult a health professional. Often referred to an ENT specialist, the absence of a physiological deficit is often the first tangible clinical sign of an autistic disorder. Around the second year of life, parents begin to appreciate the subtleties and nuances of these "hearing problems". These problems are often irregular and selective. Although the human voice seems to be virtually ignored, certain sounds, even very faint ones, can trigger reflexive attentional movements. What's more, certain noises can give pleasure to the subject and lead to addictive and stereotyped behaviour. Conversely, others can be completely unbearable for the subject, particularly in the case of hyper-acusis.

Studies and testimonies also reveal that patients with autism have a certain difficulty in establishing effective selectivity in the face of ambient noise. What is known today as the *cocktail party effect*[23] , which enables a subject to inhibit most of the interfering stimuli in a noisy situation, in order to focus on the relevant information, seems to be cruelly lacking in this population. In a noisy environment, even clearly enunciated words will be extremely interfered with and probably misunderstood by the subject. The difficulty of maintaining attention in such conditions is bound to lead to severe fatigue and an increased need for time to discriminate and process information.

3.1.2. The vision

The specificities of vision in autistic children are less obvious than those of hearing. In addition to the hyper-sensitivity to light that can be observed in the obvious manifestations of pain and discomfort, other more subtle phenomena have been brought to light by the accounts of autistic people themselves. They tell us that there may be as many ways of perceiving reality visually as there are autistic people: flat perception in two dimensions, aura or highlight effect, blurring of contours, synaesthetic perception, visualisation of abstract ideas.

One of the most important points concerning the impact of visual perception on autistic children concerns food. The visual aspect of food, its colours, textures and even packaging are crucial elements in determining the child's eating behaviour.

We should also mention visual self-stimulation, which can lead to major health problems. Some autistic people seek to impose on themselves sometimes extreme intensities of light, by looking

---

[23] Cherry, E.C. (1953). Some experiments on the recognition of speech with one and two ears, *Journal of the Acoustical Society of America*, 25.

closely at light bulbs, or even worse at the sun. Some subjects are also observed to exert pressure on the cornea through the eyelid in order to generate coloured spots in front of the eyes. As in the case of addictive behaviours linked to hearing, here the sensory organ sees its informative dimension completely negated in favour of self-directed stimulation. These various forms of self-stimulation, as well as leading to social isolation, can also, in extreme cases, cause malaise or epileptic seizures.

3.1.3. Taste and smell

We have dealt with these two meanings together because it seems to us that they are intimately linked from both a functional and representational point of view.

Some autistic patients use their sense of smell to make their first assessment of an unfamiliar object. This applies to both things and people, and is undoubtedly an extremely undesirable behaviour in the social sphere. Even when they learn to inhibit this behaviour, these subjects remain highly sensitive to odours, sometimes even the faintest ones. Anecdotally, we quote Gunilla Gerland, who confides: *"I thought there was a funny smell coming from the chair a long time after someone got up and didn't want me to sit in it [...]. But it wasn't a good idea to tell them, because then they'd come up to sniff and confidently say: "It doesn't smell anything in here". So I preferred not to sit down"*[24] .

On the other hand, some patients show a liking for smells that are commonly considered strong, which they may sometimes seem to enjoy to the detriment of their immediate environment. Certain solvents and paints can be very popular scents. Genital-anal odours are also sometimes sought after.

The mouth can also be an organ for discovering new objects. While this can be seen as a simple developmental factor, during which the child apprehends reality through this medium rather than with his or her hands, these behaviours can also have an autistic specificity. Indeed, these subjects sometimes show an unusual attraction for tastes such as bitter and salty. In addition, taste discovery is often a problem associated with autism, and many parents report the extent to which their children's menus are limited, often both quantitatively and qualitatively. Naoki Higashida, for example, reports that he has to taste a food many times before he can distinguish its taste subtleties[25] . He urges parents to repeat their attempts to get their autistic children to taste new foods so that they have time to appreciate them.

This raises the question of malnutrition and undernutrition, as autistic children can be totally resistant to nutrition. What's more, the feeling of hunger, which is rarely communicated (rarely felt?), makes it difficult for those around them to manage meals.

3.1.4. Touch

The sensory aspects associated with touch in autism essentially take the form of an unpleasant

---

[24] Gerland, G. (2004). Une personne à part entière. Mougins: Autisme France Diffusion.
[25] Higashida, N. (2007). Sais-tu pourquoi je saute? (trans. D. Mitchell & D. Roche). Paris: Les arènes.

hyperesthesia that generates anxiety. It seems, moreover, that it is mainly fine touches that are experienced as unpleasant by these subjects. According to testimonies such as that of Temple Grandin, a light touch can provoke such a strong sensation that only withdrawal and excessive vestibular stimulation can calm it down. One of the notable consequences of this state of affairs concerns the family sphere, given the obvious emotional implications of refusing gentle contact (kissing, caressing). Hyperesthesia is even more pronounced in certain areas of the body, such as the skin, teeth, ear canal, navel and genitals. This hyper-sensitivity makes care difficult and sometimes has disastrous implications, such as the impossibility of trimming the nails of a child who uses them to mutilate himself.

In our experience with autistic children, we have noticed that prolonged support over large areas of the body can, even more than not disturbing the child, provide a certain pleasure and lead to relative ataraxia. It would seem that such pressure could also have an impact on auditory thresholds. One of the most famous examples is that of Temple Grandin who, inspired by the cattle traps used by farmers to immobilise their animals in a certain tranquillity, designed a *"squeezing machine"*[26] enabling him to modulate pressure on large parts of the body. This pressure, and the anticipation of its intensity, enabled her to regain her composure and silence. Many parents tell us that they wedge their children between a bolster and the wall, which they believe soothes them and helps them fall asleep, and there are now orthopaedic devices on the market which, thanks to an assembly of firm foam cylinders, can accommodate the child in a confined space. On an anecdotal basis, we would simply point out that the packing technique is very similar to these methods, although it has been criticised, which seems to us to be due more to ideological leanings towards psychoanalysis than to any real danger posed by the procedure.

Strangely, some autistic children may be hypo-sensitive to stimuli that anyone would find unpleasant.

3.1.5. Heat and pain

Among the sensations generally considered to be intense that autistic patients do not seem to perceive normally, heat is the first that we will look at. While many patients show a complete inability to manage their personal temperature and adapt their clothing to climatic conditions, there are more serious examples of perceptive failure with regard to heat.

During an outdoor lunch with her family, Léa grabbed the barbecue grill with her bare hands, without even sawing, and of course without using the handles. The first three layers of skin remained on the grill and had to be removed from her hands. Neither during the treatment nor during the healing period did she show the slightest sign of pain. She simply had to be prevented from scratching the scarring crusts that formed and itched when the process was over.

---

[26] Grandin T (1994) Ma vie d'autiste Odile Jacob : Paris

The issue of pain in autistic patients is highly problematic, as they have a very high tolerance of pain, and also have difficulty identifying and expressing it. This can obviously have serious health consequences, particularly in the case of non-visible disorders for which pain would have been the first tangible sign.

3.1.6. Sensory self-stimulation

The question of self-stimulation is a cross-cutting one when we talk about the sensory dimension of autism. The vestibular system, linked to a structure close to the inner ear called the rochus, manages information about balance and the position of the head in relation to the body, in particular, but also in relation to horizontal and vertical reference points in the environment. The rocking movements typical of autism and the repeated movements of the head are exhilarating forms of vestibular stimulation that enable them to escape from environmental constraints that are perceived as threatening.

Skin stimulation can also be very prevalent, depending on the individual, causing serious lesions whose healing processes lead the subject into a vicious circle of compulsive scratching.

Lastly, genital stimulation is quite often observed, and it appears to be the exploitation of an area rich in sensory sensors, and therefore very satisfying from a perceptual point of view, rather than the genital fulfilment of structured sexual fantasies. In little girls, such as Léa, we sometimes witness the vulva rubbing against the floor or an object through movements of the pelvis, which can lead to more or less serious irritation if repeated too often. In young boys, it is often initially a case of the foreskin rolling over the glans, without there appearing to be any successive masturbatory movements. During puberty, this type of movement can occur and can cause significant problems when the subject is unable to achieve his goals, sometimes because he does not know what they are.

Finally, we would like to point out that, in contrast to stimulation processes, there are protective and filtering behaviours that can be observed when children put their hands over their ears or eyes, in order to distance themselves as quickly as possible from an overwhelming stimulus.

3.1.7. Critical reasoning and clinical recommendations

We have deliberately set out and listed in detail the sensory aspects of autism in order to show just how central and pervasive they can be in this condition. We have chosen to focus on this aspect of the disease rather than its motor dimension, which, although disorders also appear on the motor side (particularly in terms of the level of motor activity, tone, posture, gait and clumsiness). We do not deny the importance of this, and it seems that these two types of disorder are even particularly linked. However, it was rather the sensory dimension that struck us during our placement and which helped us to explain the phenomena that follow.

We postulate that stereotyped movements, while certainly constituting a motor discharge, are sought above all for their sensory value. This afferential internality was explained above. To illustrate this point, we will take the example of Léa. She used to flap her arms frantically, which often ended up throwing her off balance. By repeatedly suggesting various movements and showing her by example, the team and ourselves worked for several months to change this stereotypy, which was such a problem on a daily basis. However, Léa didn't seem to be interested in any other movement and kept repeating the same series of gestures over and over again. Finally, we succeeded in shifting this stereotypy to applause. Since then, Léa has joined her wrists together and clapped her hands when the compulsion seizes her. It's certainly not a victory, but the merit of this diversion is that it solved the problem of imbalance. It seems to us that the simple fact that it is possible to vary the motor manifestation of stereotypy by proposing a variant of the same sensory nature, when other proposals have failed, demonstrates that the sensory value of the action is primordial here.

By taking this approach, we could adapt the treatment of autism by giving priority to the sensory pathways so that, even if we do not cure the subject, we enable a better understanding. To do this, we need to recognise the dimension of suffering that the sensory sphere can represent for the subject in order to limit it, but also the need that the autistic person may have to experience and feel it, as Gunilla Gerland tells us: "*I was trying, from the sensory point of view, a very logical and creative way of controlling my suffering*"[27] .

The question of body schema also seems to us to need to be taken very seriously. First of all, we can think of stereotyped movements as a physical-sensory exploration of the limits of the body and its positioning. As we refined our thinking, we came up with the idea that it was possible that the movements in question were performed precisely to self-stimulate hypo-sensitive parts of the body. As we explained above, Léa showed hypo-sensitivity to heat in her hands, which her third-degree burn will certainly not have improved. We might therefore wonder whether the reason for the flapping and clapping movements might be to raise awareness in a part of the body that the subject is somehow aware of being underdeveloped. By association of ideas with the notion of sensitisation, it seems legitimate to us to think that by applying habituation processes modelled on autistic logic, while diverting the objects, we could achieve some clinical result.

There is still a great deal to be explored in terms of the clinical treatment of autism, and we need to take advantage of the proliferation of ideas in this area to develop the therapies of tomorrow.

Neuroscience is an important and promising avenue here. Recent advances in rTMS (repeated Transcranial Magnetic Stimulation) and tDCS (transcranial Direct Current Stimulation) are relatively promising. The use of these techniques on the areas involved in autistic pathology enables artificial regulation of inhibitory and excitatory neurotransmission systems, the effects of which have

---

[27] Gerland, G. (2004). Une personne à part entière. Mougins: Autisme France Diffusion.

already been observed. We can therefore imagine a future in which autism will benefit from a range of experimentally validated treatments, and in which the various players in the medical and psychological sectors will be able to combine treatments and obtain satisfactory results.

3.2. The phenomenon of autistic regression

In this section, we will distinguish two forms of autistic regression: one primary, the other (or others) secondary. The first form relates to the onset of autism itself, when the first signs of autism become apparent and a reversal of the subject's developmental pattern is perceived. It may also be linked to certain pathways of entry into the pathology, which may take the form of an epileptic seizure, stroke, coma, cranial trauma, and so on. Clinical experience shows that many autistic children have had such a potentially developmentally disruptive event prior to their pathology. Following this, a phenomenon of regression in development was observed, influencing most aspects of the subject's life.

The second type of regression concerns all those that occur in the course of the autistic patient's life and which constitute so many steps backwards in the progress and acquisitions made. Although distressing for family and friends, these regressions nevertheless tell us something about the autistic child's subjective experience. While we certainly have no miracle solution to offer, we nonetheless thought it would be interesting to give an account of these questions and the hypotheses that have occurred to us.

3.2.1. Primary regression

The common nosography (DSM IV-TR) distinguishes two forms of autism, in terms of the onset of the pathology. The first, Kanner-type autism, or precocious infantile autism, presents a clinical picture that is immediately evident in the first year of life. The second, known as regressive autism or acquired autistic disorder, involves a generally normal development, followed in the second or third year of life by regression in many aspects of development, such as language, mimicry, attention, cleanliness, interest in the environment, and so on. It must be said, however, that some mild developmental deficits may have gone undetected despite their presence. In the case of primary regression, it is mainly the sphere of relationships and language skills that are affected by this developmental setback, and it is possible that because of the young age of the subject, certain mild signs may have been missed.

In some cases, the environmental and traumatic pathway is relevant, when a very strong and significant event occurs before the regression leading to autism. A little boy we know, Tanh, was hit by a car at the age of three. After a normal start to his development and an entry into language that augured well for the future, he showed a complete regression in language, accompanied by a calm and distant mutism. His social interactions also came to a complete halt, and he began to develop typical autistic symptoms (withdrawal, stereotypies, avoidance of eye contact, obsessions, etc.).

40

Although the doctors who have been treating him since then say that there are no brain scars as a result of the shock, and that on an MRI scan he appears to have no problems, the fact remains that the boy presents a complete symptomatology consistent with autism. In this case in particular, it is possible to ask the question of the impact of strong life events, particularly from an emotional and sensory point of view, on the ongoing development of a young subject.

The phenomenon of primary regression also applies to Rett syndrome, in which it can occur very late (up to the age of 4). Thereafter, the autistic picture becomes more pronounced, and physical symptoms such as difficulties with locomotion and strange body proportions linked to motor disorders are added. It should be noted, however, that this disease is primarily linked to cerebral atrophy and proven genetic causes (it only affects girls).

There are many debates surrounding this obvious setback in children's development, and etiological controversies pit the proponents of an environmental origin against those of a neuro-genetic etiopathogenesis. Whatever the answer to this debate, it is important to note that, ultimately, the developmental stages of autistic children can be influenced by appropriate methods. This simple fact, proven by therapists of all kinds and by autistic people whose testimonies are increasingly numerous, allows us to glimpse a clinical horizon which is not necessarily determined by a neuro-developmental linearity which is sterile from an operational point of view.

3.2.2. Secondary regressions

This is what we call the phases of regression that occur in the development of diagnosed autistic children. The main question remains how to explain this puzzling phenomenon, which, as far as we know, is present in many non-verbal autistic children.

It is understood that a certain number of abilities are intended to develop during the second year of life, after a certain amount of maturation. If this maturation is disrupted, we sometimes see a deterioration in the acquisitions made. Uta Frith, a developmental psychologist at the Institute of Cognitive Neuroscience at University College London and a specialist in autism, has put forward a hypothesis about these phenomena that we find extremely interesting. She proposes an analogy between the secondary regressions of autism and those observed during the normal development of the child, when a skill appears early but is not really functional. One example is assisted walking or early imitation: these can be seen in newborns only a few days old, before they disappear completely, only to be mobilised again after various successive stages leading to their emergence and completion. According to Uta Frith, the primary forms of language initially disappear in normal children, allowing the more complex processes of true language to emerge. In the case of non-verbal regressive autism, this first stage of extinction would lead to the complete disappearance of language skills.

Regressive phenomena are all the more salient in forms of autism associated with epilepsy.

41

Representing between 15% and 30% of cases of autism, epileptic co-morbidity subjects the subject to critical tensions which have a considerable immediate effect on the state of the illness. As a result, some autistic people progressively regress through repeated epileptic episodes, each time more profound, and accumulate a mental retardation that can prove highly incapacitating.

In order to focus on clinical phenomena within our remit, we have chosen to look at *a priori* spontaneous regressions, i.e. those which do not follow any epileptic episode. To do this, we will again look at the case of Éléonore, aged 7.

During our placement, we observed a twofold change in this patient's behaviour. On the one hand, she began to show more and more interest in others, to make eye contact and to use complex expressions for which she practised caricaturally in the mirror; she became more and more attracted to abstract and communicative objects such as letters and words, which she timidly began to pronounce in her fluent voice, gradually entering the realm of language. Abandoning some of her more confining stereotypies, she showed increasing interest in the activities of others, often joining in and even imitating them. On the other hand, during the same period she showed two distinct regressive phenomena. At times, she once again showed great distress and wept in a way she had never done before, and she also went back several years in terms of the cleanliness she had acquired. In fact, the number of 'accidents' increased, and Éléonore now refused to relieve herself when taken to the toilet. This never fails to alarm the parents and fuel the fears of those around her!

A number of ideas came to mind that might help us to understand the nature and reasons for this regression, and have the merit of providing explanations *in vivo*, in the subject's lived experience.

First of all, we were struck by the potentially exploratory nature of urinating and defecating on oneself, particularly in terms of the sensory experience of the sphincters. In fact, this forgetfulness of cleanliness coincides with regular and repeated digital exploration of the vulva and anus. It might therefore be thought that these new sensations and the new awareness of an intense sensory zone could somehow disrupt the muscular gains linked to the sphincters. In this case, it is highly likely that cleanliness will return with the habituation of the sensations linked to this area, which for the moment are interfering with the sensory-motor activity linked to retention.

We noted above the correlation between difficulties with cleanliness and a new awareness of otherness. It was on this basis, and taking into account the character of the subject, that we developed our second idea. Éléonore is a child who, if you look closely, has a very strong fear of others, and a major reluctance to interact. This shyness is particularly apparent in the very rare moments when she speaks. This is done in an almost inaudible voice, the antithesis of her usual repetitive high-pitched voicing. On the basis of this shyness, and her recent awareness of otherness, it appeared to us that the little girl might suffer from a certain embarrassment about relieving herself in front of a third party. Admittedly, this would represent a considerable advance in the development of care, and we naturally

42

remain cautious. However, we recommended at the meeting that they should try to leave her alone to go to the toilet, or at least that someone other than her carer should take her there, in order to create a break and a specific moment. Trainees in childcare make this possible.

Finally, it was the very nature of this development that led us to our third idea: bidirectional, both regressive in terms of cleanliness and positive in terms of the development of complex abilities such as language and taking others into account. For a child who was so withdrawn into her own world, such progress is considerable, and it would be unreasonable to deny the cognitive load and emotional investment that such a process represents. We therefore postulate that the integration of new skills can take place at the expense of acquired abilities that suddenly become inoperative. In this case, cleanliness, which she may no longer have been paying attention to, would have been disrupted by the burden represented in all respects by the new acquisitions. It seems to us that this effect of communicating vessels could sometimes help to understand the phenomena of secondary regression occurring in autistic patients who are otherwise making progress. When we observe a secondary regression, we should ask ourselves questions and observe the child to find out whether another aptitude is developing at the same time, which needs to be taken into account and supported.

3.4. Asperger's syndrome

Asperger's syndrome, being a special case of autistic pathology, needs to be explained in greater detail. Able to express themselves and not mentally retarded, these subjects nevertheless suffer from many of the problems associated with autism. We were particularly interested to see how an intellectually high-functioning mind perceived itself when confronted with complex disorders linked to sometimes unspeakable aspects of consciousness. We also looked at the question of so-called high-functioning autistic subjects, which we will discuss later.

In order to understand this disorder, which is well documented and supported by the testimonies of people suffering from the syndrome, we are going to use the case of a young man in our care who was diagnosed in this way.

3.4.1. Antonio's clinical case

Antonio is a 10-year-old boy of South American origin with a form of verbal autism of the Asperger's type. He was diagnosed at a very early stage and cared for in a facility applying the ABA method. He is currently at school with the help of an educational assistant. Discussions	mediocre. If he has no difficulties with grammar or spelling, he seems to have to make a major effort to focus his attention on a text. He quickly slips into periods of absence from which it is almost impossible to escape. He responds fairly well to the demands of

are underway to enable him to attend school on his own from next year. His profile is fairly typical for someone with Asperger's syndrome. He has emotional difficulties and does not adapt well to public life. Difficult to socialise with, he has few friends and is often mocked. But this doesn't seem to affect him too much. Highly inquisitive by nature, he has a fertile imagination and inner life. He is interested in all new knowledge, with a particular fondness for insects. There's also a certain morbid obsession with technical disasters, particularly rail ones. Very independent, they are nevertheless very communicative and at ease with adults. He has no trouble concentrating on the activities he prefers. At school, he excels in maths and science, while his reading and writing skills are very good.	everyday life and to authority and its agents, despite tantrums that are no different from those of any other child. Until he was 7, he had stereotyped movements and swaying, which eventually disappeared after becoming progressively rarer. Today he is essentially obsessed with certain textures, words and sounds, which seem to have a power that is sometimes hypnotic and sometimes euphoric. When confronted with these objects, he sometimes complains that he can't get them out of his head. It also has a strong attraction for major vestibular and proprioceptive stimuli such as thrill rides. On the whole, he's a cheerful, pleasant young man, with whom you can spend some very rewarding moments, and who has a very interesting capacity for self-analysis.

3.4.2. Social difficulties

The social life of patients with Asperger's syndrome suffers from a number of complex difficulties linked to a variety of factors.

Firstly, some of them are linked to the disease itself and the clinical signs that can be observed by anyone.

The most glaring example we saw in Antonio was his failure to understand and integrate certain social conventions. For example, the young boy has difficulty grasping that it is not acceptable to belch or flatter in public, and fails to apply the most basic rules of politeness consistently. In fact, it seems that in autistic people, the internalisation of social norms and etiquette is compromised. This is also what Gunilla Gerland tells us, when she explains why she didn't reach out to other people during her childhood: "To *tell the truth, it wasn't that I gave up trying to console myself with other people, it just never occurred to me that anyone could do it*"[28] . This failure to internalise social norms and conventions generally provokes reactions of incomprehension in those around him, linked to a feeling of strangeness and indifference, and this is indeed what we saw with Antonio, who very often finds

---

[28] Gerland, G. (2004). Une personne à part entière. Mougins: Autisme France Diffusion.

himself excluded.

The tendency of people with Asperger's to become absorbed in certain objects can also distance them from the social sphere, and vex, bore or annoy those around them. During interactions themselves, a certain lack of finesse in anticipating the intentions and state of mind of others can be very disconcerting and embarrassing. Difficulties in understanding humour, an undeniable vector of social cohesion, deprive them of the opportunity to take part in many group situations. On a broader level, their lack of ability to perceive abstraction and express emotions means that they are often difficult to communicate with, despite their undeniable language skills. Finally, a certain social naivety can sometimes confine them to the role of whipping boy, leading them to prefer avoidance in order to protect themselves. The freedom of action and decision-making of some people with Asperger's syndrome, combined with the tolerance sometimes shown by the institutions that take them in, can also generate a feeling of jealousy among their peers, which further encourages their ostracism.

Patients with autism also face other social difficulties, which stem from factors linked to the management of autism itself. We will therefore focus on this last aspect.

Since it was recognised as a disability at national level, treatment methods for this pathology have developed considerably and, while they have undeniable benefits, they nevertheless entail certain disadvantages in terms of the patient's social life. In our opinion, regular psycho-educational follow-up of a patient results in a modification (however slight) of certain aspects of identity and subjectivity. As we saw with Antonio, some forms of treatment are very demanding in terms of intensity and duration. The impression of abnormality that such care can provoke in these patients is also reinforced by the reduced autonomy and sense of dependence that it induces. It seems to us that self-confidence can be undermined by treatment that affects all areas of the patient's life. In addition, a certain dependence on support can develop, which needs to be taken into account if the patient is ultimately to be able to manage his or her own life. What's more, their daily lives are very different from those of their peers. On the one hand, this care is extremely time-consuming, and compliance with established protocols necessarily limits certain normal activities (outings with peers, group games, invitations to birthdays, and so on). Any parent will admit that, in order to comply with the requirements of monitoring, the child's social life regularly has to be deprived of many moments that would otherwise have been enjoyable. On the other hand, the methodical and systematic protocolisation that we have observed for Antonio with the ABA method seems to us to disempower the subject and lead him to focus his interest on the rewards obtained for performing the expected behaviours, to the detriment of an understanding of their raison d'être, which we feel would be more lasting. Of course, explaining the reasons for a behaviour is not enough to ensure that it is carried out, but it is still necessary to mention them so that the subject can anchor them permanently in their system of thought and action.

The social aspect of autism care that we would now like to mention concerns a measure that is dependent on the French State: the mobilisation of Aides de Vie Scolaire (AVS) which, we do not deny, has many advantages, but also has limitations which, to our knowledge, are very little taken into account and relayed. The presence of these carers in the classroom means that the reason for their presence has to be explained to the other children and their parents beforehand. In addition, the use of video equipment recommended by the most widespread methods (TEACCH and ABA) requires parents to sign a special form. In our opinion, all these precautions focused on a single child lead to a significant stigmatisation of people with Asperger's syndrome. Young people are not particularly recognised for their tenderness in groups, and the visibility of the AVSs acts as an obvious stigma highlighting the abnormality of the patient in their care. It also seems to us that the presence of AVSs during extracurricular activities is not necessarily beneficial. Subjects with Asperger's have a certain tendency to prefer the calm and rationality of adults rather than the impulsiveness and activity of the playground, which leads them to stay with their teacher rather than try to integrate into the group. Finally, we have observed that, although motivated by laudable intentions, the specific treatment received by children with Asperger's syndrome creates a feeling of injustice among their peers, which often results in their rejection.

Far from wishing to criticise this type of care, whose benefits are obvious, we wanted to show its limits, because we believe that by refining certain aspects it would be possible to achieve a form of care with less social impact, given that these patients are already experiencing significant difficulties in this area.

3.4.3. Cognitive aspects of Asperger's syndrome

Because people with this syndrome have good language and reasoning skills, it is interesting to question this specificity in order to understand the links that exist between autistic symptoms and the cognitive sphere.

Obsessions may appear to be invasive, but they can be seen in a different light. The young Antonio whose case we have described has an inordinate and obsessive interest in (mainly) two distinct subjects: insects and technical disasters. While these very strong interests may tend towards excess, they are no less fruitful in *the end*. Antonio's intellectual and memory skills have given him a highly developed knowledge of these subjects, which he understands in great detail. His curiosity, which is always focused on subjects in which he has this kind of obsessive interest, leads him to ask many questions, the answers to which he devours insatiably in order to expand his knowledge. In this case, while it should be noted that this thirst for knowledge does not seem to generate anxiety, the obsessive nature of autism ultimately enables functional, long-term learning, and even strong areas of expertise. What's more, it acts as a palliative to the attentional difficulties encountered when faced with objects of limited interest. Another characteristic of autism is the social isolation we mentioned earlier. While we would not venture to claim that such isolation can be intrinsically positive, it does have certain consequences which are not at all untoward. These subjects often use the time they save by distancing themselves from others to cultivate their knowledge and perfect their learning. It's often in contact with an adult that they have the opportunity to talk about subjects that interest them, and thus have social interactions that, although not of their own age, are very real indeed.

One of the main limitations of the cognitive abilities of patients with Asperger's syndrome is that they can act as a screen for the care of the subject. We know that, like other forms of autism, Asperger's syndrome involves a number of perceptual and sensory problems which have a considerable impact on subjective experience and development. The verbal skills of these subjects, and their thirst to feed a sometimes abundant cognitive sphere, sometimes mask deeper difficulties. What's more, despite their mastery of language, they have difficulty expressing their feelings and emotions, which makes it all the more difficult to detect underlying problems. We therefore need to pay close attention to any non-verbal manifestations of these problems, and tailor our monitoring to the issues identified. To do this, it will be necessary to go beyond the language aspects and use them.

3.4.4. High-functioning autistic people

First of all, we would like to make it clear that the term used is somewhat overused. Neither the DSM-IV TR nor the ICD-10 use it or deal with the reality that it refers to. We understand high-level autism not simply as opposed to severe autism, but as the simultaneous manifestation of autistic signs and one or more cognitive abilities pushed to the extreme. Common thinking often lumps together Asperger's syndrome and high-functioning autism. However, it is not correct to assert that people with Asperger's syndrome all have particularly developed abilities in a given area. On the other hand, it should be noted that these subjects do exist and have a number of impressive characteristics. We will therefore call them high-functioning autistic people.

Although they have an autistic clinical picture, they also have extraordinary predispositions that far exceed the limits usually accepted. Although we have not met any such individuals, there is a vast literature on the subject, the fruit of the enthusiasm of professionals and individuals for the fabulous dispositions they display.

Some of these subjects have an eidetic memory which, thanks to a holistic processing of information, enables them to acquire information extremely quickly and to reproduce it flawlessly. Another can reproduce from memory, with a very high degree of reliability, the details of an urban landscape over which it has only briefly flown. Another will be capable of amazing feats in algebra, or at the piano. It seems that these individuals have an inordinate passion for a particular field, and through their obsessions with it, manage to acquire extreme knowledge and skills. However, they display a number of autistic traits. The first of these is impaired social skills. Recognising faces can be difficult, as can understanding facial expressions and non-verbal language in general. Affectivity and emotions are problematic, and these patients have difficulty both in identifying and expressing their own emotions and in understanding and adapting to those of others. In some cases, there are also praxis difficulties, which can be significant. As a result, they may need support and assistance on a day-to-day basis. Some everyday tasks are potentially impossible, and their exceptional abilities are useless. This idea of total expertise coupled with major difficulties in autonomy has led researchers to question the notion of genius, to find out whether there could be a link between certain forms of autism and the great minds of our history. While these cases are very rare, they do teach us something about the cost of increased cognitive capacity and the complexity of human understanding.

CHAPTER 4

4. Practical realities

4.1. Reflections on the concept of diagnosis

The question of diagnosis raises a number of issues that are complexly intertwined and multifaceted. Obediences, movements of thought, types of care structure, all have an influence on diagnostic reasoning, its construction, its aims and its consequences. We set out to understand the determinants of diagnostic reasoning and its value to our subject, given that diagnosis is the focal point of any approach to mental disorders in our societies.

4.1.1. Adrien's clinical case

Adrien is a young boy of 9, and is a rather special case we met during our course. Initially diagnosed as psychotic by an IME and a CMP previously consulted (we have no further information), he was subsequently diagnosed with both autism and ADHD, and placed on Ritalin. Outside the school system, he receives lessons as best he can from his mother, in the mornings for 2 hours, at home.

One of Adrien's main problems is physical violence. He is extremely brutal towards most of the people he comes into contact with, and presents a profile close to the clinical picture of dyssocial personalities with heteroaggressive violence.

This is a boy who speaks very well, is very talkative, and has a clear ability to manipulate those around him. He understands the dynamics of a given situation very well, knows how to adapt to it, and when the stakes are high enough (such as when the social services come to his home) he is able to smooth out his constantly in the eyes, does not show any stereotyped behaviour, or even any withdrawal whatsoever, and does not display any particular sensory sensitivity (as described in *3.2. Sensory aspects of the disease*).

The sessions with him are very lively, to say the least, and most of the time Adrien is extremely authoritarian and tries to direct the proceedings himself. He generally wants to involve the counsellor in role-playing around a morbid imagination of his own (stories of bandits, murderers, prison, etc). He forces the other person to disguise themselves, does the same, and constantly tries to enforce his decisions. In the midst of all this, there are moments of great brutality, in the face of which the caregiver's physical and emotional withdrawal often seems to lead to a fear of abandonment that remains central to the subject's problems. The dependence he has developed on otherness is, in our view, far removed from the autistic profile and reality.

49

behaviour considerably in order to meet the demands of the moment and take advantage of them. Compared to the other patients at the Lud'éveil centre, he is very different. He looks	The difficulty in treating this patient lies in their cognitive development, which sometimes masks primary problems, and more generally, in our view, in their mismatch with the autistic profile.

4.1.2. Comorbidities

The co-morbidities associated with autism require the practitioner to understand how the patient's pathology is structured, and the extent to which the associated phenomena influence follow-up. They vary from one patient to another, but it is possible to isolate some of the most common ones.

Epilepsy, with a prevalence ranging from one-fifth to one-third of the autistic population, depending on the study, is a major comorbidity. During our placement, two of the five patients undergoing intensive follow-up had epilepsy. In both cases, we were told that a major seizure had occurred in the first few months of life, significantly altering cerebral function and development. The presence of forms of epilepsy in autism accentuates certain disorders and their onset, such as anxiety linked to the fear of seizures, or the secondary regression that can occur after seizures. In addition, there may be a link between epilepsy and the mental retardation observed in these patients.

In fact, mental retardation is a second comorbidity. While it is true that the specific determinants of autism have obvious consequences for learning ability and intellectual capacity, it seems to us that in some cases very severe mental retardation may be wrongly associated with autism. However, mental retardation is mainly seen in language inability, which is, after all, the best indicator of developments in conceptual and symbolic understanding.

Anxieties are also important, but very difficult to treat. Although interventions based on the sensory aspects of subjective experience can lead to some satisfactory results, language deficits make it difficult to understand these anxieties and the reasons for them. The practitioner must therefore adopt a highly developed observational stance, in order to pick up on the slim indicators that give a glimpse of the causes of these anxieties. They can be very strong, generating self-aggressive and sometimes hetero-aggressive behaviour, and are extremely trying for patients, who lose a great deal of their energy and willpower.

Attention deficit disorder and hyperactivity are also potential co-morbidities. Obvious in some hypertonic autistic patients, it may be more difficult to detect in others, for whom it is not manifested in a motor way, but by an internal overload and tension sometimes visible in stereotyped behaviour. These various co-morbidities are by no means an exhaustive list, but simply a reminder of the disorders associated with and contained in autism that we were able to observe during our placement, and which we feel would benefit patients and their care if taken into account. These co-morbidities can lead to hesitations about the diagnosis, particularly in the case of verbal autistic patients, which is why it is necessary to identify them and take them into account when assessing and monitoring patients.

4.1.3. Social and representational aspects

The notion of a diagnosis has many determining factors. During our placement, we were led to reflect on these issues and to understand that there is nothing trivial about formulating a diagnosis. In fact, it inevitably responds to causes which, directly and indirectly, shape and influence it.

As mentioned earlier, autism was recognised as a specific disability in 1996. This has several implications. First of all, the fact that it has this status means that care can be provided on a psycho-educational basis rather than on a medical-psychological basis, as is the case for mental illnesses. In addition, the public budgets allocated to associations and institutions dealing with people with disabilities are considerably higher. It is also important to note that, on an individual basis, this status provides privileged access to care, thanks to full coverage by the social security system, as well as substantial social benefits. Without in any way claiming that diagnoses of autism can be made by connivance and self-interested calculations, the fact remains that the factors we have just mentioned must be important.

The broadening of the diagnostic criteria set out in the DSM-IV TR and V has also changed the operational reality of autistic diagnosis. Now that the notion of a spectrum is officially accepted, this has led to an inevitable and meteoric rise in the number of patients diagnosed in this way.

The arrival in the 1990s of American movements of thought concerning the care and treatment of autism led to the increasingly virulent questioning of psychoanalytical theories on autism. The idea of a dysfunction in the mother-child relationship has gradually been supplanted by the theory of a neurodevelopmental disorder, a direction that we believe is leading to a profound change in the perception and representations associated with the nosographic entity of autism. Since mothers are no longer directly to blame, we can legitimately assume that this makes it easier for the practitioner to state the diagnosis and for the family to accept it. Indeed, we often see parents going from facility to facility, from practitioner to practitioner, until the diagnosis is made that 'suits them', that they are capable of admitting, and which will constitute the future pathological reality of their child, obviously determining the care that will be provided. The new methods of caring for autistic patients, which include parents, also seem to us to encourage acceptance of the diagnosis.

Finally, the common imagination has evolved a great deal on the subject of autism and popular culture has taken hold of the subject. In the cinema, in bookshops, on television and on the radio, autism is often presented in the most favourable light, and there are countless programmes reporting on the intellectual exploits of some autistic people. While it is true that the day-to-day realities of non-verbal autistic people are often kept quiet, the increase in popular representations of verbal autistic people has led to a less dramatic appraisal of the condition itself. These developments seem to us to be of undoubted importance in the process leading to the establishment, statement and acceptance of a diagnosis of autism.

As we explained earlier, Adrien's mother first consulted professionals at an IME and a CMP, both of whom mentioned psychotic disorders. In her own words, Adrien's mother "couldn't stand it" when people said her son was psychotic. She therefore decided to go to hospitals until her son was diagnosed with autism. However, in view of the subject's lack of progress in the treatment adapted to the autism from which he has benefited for two and a half years at the Lud'éveil centre, as well as the increase in his anxieties and his heteroaggressive acts, and finally the total absence of clinical signs consistent with autism, it seems to us that in this particular case the establishment of this diagnosis is highly prejudicial to the patient. In fact, if the mention of psychosis is relevant, its denial will have led to the wrong therapeutic orientation. On the other hand, current common representations of psychosis and autism enable us to understand why Adrien's mother preferred the latter terminology. In short, it seems to us that certain social determinants can lead, as in this case, to misjudgements with potentially disastrous long-term consequences. It is the practitioner's responsibility to temper the prejudices of the patient's entourage so that a diagnosis can be established that is as much as possible the fruit of observation of the clinical signs and study of the anamnesis, rather than that of social and societal considerations regarding this or that pathology.

4.1.4. Institutional influences

The final determinant we wish to address in relation to the question of diagnosis lies in the institutional aspects.

First of all, the different branches of psychology sometimes have very different presuppositions with regard to psychological disorders, and as a result their diagnostic responses can be very different. Some concepts even have no equivalent in one system of thought or another. Take, for example, the notion of infantile psychosis, which qualifies autism from the psychoanalytical point of view, and which has no effective correspondence in the DSM, which accepts neither the notion of neurosis nor the notion of psychosis. We can also draw a parallel between the considerations of supporters of neurobiological aetiology and those of psychoanalysts, which boil down to a debate on nature versus nurture. Despite all the advances in science, the latter remains at the heart of the debate on autism. It is inevitable that such divergences will influence the practitioner's assessment of the patient and the diagnosis itself, as well as the follow-up recommended.

The structures used to provide care also seem to have an influence on diagnosis. It's true that there is a correlation between theoretical persuasions and places of care, but even more so it seems that there is a kind of sociology of diagnosis. As Thomas J. Scheff showed in his book <u>Being mentally ill: a sociological theory</u> (1966), on the subject of schizophrenia and bipolar disorders, it seems that the type of care structure has a considerable influence on diagnostic tendencies. In addition, the type of patient, their social level, cultural background and ethnic group could also have an impact. In this way, we can think of diagnosis as the result of a succession of assessments of various criteria, the adequacy of which leads to a given direction. While this is not a restrictive approach, it is important to be aware of it so as not to fall into the pitfalls of human automatisms, which are nevertheless natural. While in no way denying the fact of culture and its impact on mental illness, we simply advocate that its modalities be known, controlled and anticipated.

The last institutional aspect linked to the notion of diagnosis that we wish to deal with relates to determinants that are somewhat less noble. In the context of establishing new theories and new methods, or in order to corroborate their presuppositions, certain players in the field of autism care may have an interest in making this diagnosis for patients for whom more thought should have been given. Indeed, certain career interests may justify unscrupulous practitioners steering the diagnosis in a direction that serves their own purposes. Potentially devastating for patients and their families, these practices nevertheless exist, as we have seen for ourselves. The promotion of a system on which the reputation of the practitioner and, *de facto,* the obvious financial stakes are based, is sometimes the primary reason for making a diagnosis. We find it deplorable that such attitudes should exist among professionals who should be primarily concerned with the well-being of their patients, but who obviously prefer, sometimes with disconcerting bad faith, to adapt at all costs the theories and practices of which they are the authors.

4.2. Autism in care settings

Today, there are many facilities for autistic people, with varying degrees of specialisation. The voluntary sector in particular is teeming with initiatives aimed at caring for autistic people, and complements the public provision. The latter includes specialised day hospital services, Instituts Médico-Éducatifs (IMEs), Services d'Éducation Spéciale et de Soins à Domicile (SESSADs), Foyers d'Accueil Médicalisés (FAMs), Centres Ressources Autisme (CRAs), and Classes pour l'Inclusion Scolaire (CLISs).

The methods of care and the theoretical acceptances differ from one facility to another, and there are places where they are applied. Our aim here is to set out the limitations of some of the care we have observed. We will not go into detail about the various facilities and their specific features, but will simply focus on our experience and the questions that some of our observations have raised.

4.2.1. The Lud'Éveil 3i centre

The structure that enabled us to make the most observations was, of course, our placement site, the

Lud'éveil centre in Courbevoie, affiliated to the Autisme Espoir Vers l'École association, which applies the 3i method. To give a brief overview of how it works, the centre takes in six children, supervised six to seven days a week from 9am to 6.30pm by around forty volunteers each, who spread out throughout the week to provide play-based sessions lasting an hour and a half, which follow one another throughout the day. Although intended to be intensive, we feel that this method is perhaps a little too intensive. In fact, the children spend most of their time in the centre, and as it is difficult to know what the other participants have done with the child, and the subjects are extremely rigid about the content of their activities, the supervisors often end up doing all the same types of session, repeating the same games. Taking place in very simple rooms with just a few toys on high shelves and a frosted glass window, the time spent at Lud'éveil is not very stimulating, and ultimately seems to distance the patient from the outside world. What's more, the repetitiveness we mentioned also seems to lead to a degree of isolation. While it is true that one of the central ideas of the 3i method is to encourage the establishment of a reassuring "*cocoon*"[29] , we feel that this can reinforce the autistic problem when it takes up so much space in the patient's life, and does not include more motivating and richer proposals, or greater contact with the outside world and "real life". So what will become of their behaviour in society in the future? These children's daily lives seem to deprive them of the natural spontaneity of the world, which seems to us to reinforce their difficulty in joining the reality shared by the majority.

The nature of the support workers, who are volunteers with no training in psychology or personal assistance, also seems to us to be a major limitation. Communication between these people, mainly observed at the monthly meetings, is greatly complicated by the emotional stakes involved in each person's motivations. It can be seen that some of these people overemphasise behaviours they have observed in order to shine within the group. These biases considerably interfere with the session reports on which psychologists are supposed to base their work. The volunteers' lack of training gives them an understanding of the individual and his or her psyche that is riddled with commonplaces, urban myths and unquestioning self-righteousness. When we remember that a child treated using the 3i method spends one and a half hours a week with his psychologist and up to forty more with the volunteers, we need to consider the importance of the qualifications of those involved.

We do not wish to criticise all the work put in place by the professionals of the 3i method, because it is true that some of their proposals are quite interesting and relevant. However, we felt it necessary to point out the main limitations, while bearing in mind that this method is very new in France and that we can hope that it will be perfected in the future.

---

[29] De la Presle, C., Valeton, D. (2010). Lettres à un petit prince sorti de sa bulle: une clé pour l'autisme? Paris: L'Harmattan.

Those involved in autism care in France today are all affiliated to a given method and, consequently, to the theoretical postulates on which it is based. Each method comprises a number of techniques and tools that are used with patients. Thought of as relatively coherent internal systems, these approaches exploit the operational recommendations and theoretical advances of the obedience to which they belong. Perhaps for reasons of promotion, or perhaps for the sake of unidirectionality, it seems to us that practitioners limit the scope of their potential by restricting themselves to the contributions of the players in their theory.

It also seems to us that some methods are based on overly limited approaches and techniques. There are good ideas to be found in all these approaches, which we believe should be used in a more holistic way, free from harmful debates. One example is the contribution of psychoanalysis, which is now rejected "on principle" whenever the issue of autism is raised. In fact, we came away from our first training course meeting astonished, having heard that the 3i method claimed to be very far removed from psychoanalysis, and rejected any interpretation of this type because it clearly sought to distance itself from it. The unfortunate reputation attributed to psychoanalysis in this area has led to its authors and researchers being virtually excluded from the debate. As a result, any attempt on their part to contribute to knowledge about autism is met *ipso facto* with virulent criticism and a denial of the potential validity of the proposal. While it is undoubtedly necessary, as with any movement of thought, to sort the wheat from the chaff, it is highly probable that psychoanalysis has something to contribute to the clinic of autism, if only because it constitutes one of the principal tools for setting knowledge in motion.

In our view, the example of packing is very telling. This technique, advocated by certain psychoanalysts, involves wrapping the subject in a cold, damp, tightly-wrapped cloth to give them a sense of containment and to reinforce the feeling of the body's limits through tangible perception. We have been able to attend sessions with young autistic patients, as well as those with multiple disabilities, and it is clear that subjects suffering from extreme agitation are able to calm down and regain a clear sense of peace. However, this technique is highly criticised by autism professionals (non-psychoanalysts), who describe it as invasive and bordering on abuse. In this particular case, it is clear that it is psychoanalysis above all that is targeted by this criticism. It has to be, because we haven't seen anything that even remotely resembles abuse. On the contrary, we were very impressed by the results obtained, and found it a pity that this proposal was rejected out of hand because of its theoretical origins. This example is entirely symptomatic of the major problem we believe the autism clinic is facing today. Each method holds on to its techniques, tools and postulates, and seeks at all costs to defend and apply them, sometimes to the detriment of patients themselves. Career and promotion issues obviously play a part in this dynamic, and it is clear that the practitioners concerned have every interest in demonstrating the advantages of the method they represent.

To put it simply, most methods have obvious shortcomings. The ABA method, for example, proposes to encourage the emergence of adapted behaviours by reinforcing them (using a reinforcer chosen according to the subject) in a positive way. In our view, this has its own limitations, notably the absence of negative reinforcers, or the induction of a systematic reward logic, which is highly artificial and makes no sense in ecological conditions.

It would be possible to list the pitfalls of the different approaches, but that's not our aim. Undeniably, there are also many relevant proposals, such as imitation in the 3i method, which gives good results, the inclusion and training of parents advocated by the TEACCH method, the establishment of self-evaluated contracts in the ABA method, communication through images in the PECS method, and even packing promoted by certain psychoanalysts, or the new avenues provided by neuroscience. We hope that the autism professionals who are currently being trained and who will be practising in the future will be able to see the merits of the techniques that exist within the different approaches, and will not think that they are irreconcilable. In our view, it is clear that autism is such a complex, cross-disciplinary pathology that, in order to achieve results, it is necessary to set aside debates about posture and to know how to use the clinical tools available everywhere to build an intelligent, comprehensive approach to care.

4.2.3 On the patient's side

The reality of the care facilities we visited varied greatly from one to another. The topography, facilities and staff all have an impact on patients and their well-being. The specific nature of the disease means that we need to consider its various aspects and adapt to each patient.

Deprived of language, patients are not always able to express the reasons for the discomfort they feel, and sometimes the care staff themselves do not understand the causes. The concept of *"passive abuse"* is used (notably in the Chossy ruling of 2003)[30] to describe cases of suffering or isolation of patients who are unable to express themselves, due to ignorance, negligence or renunciation on the part of the professionals involved. In our view, this concept is particularly important in autism. To illustrate this, we can take the example of the sensory disorders encountered by the subject, which can represent an obstacle for him or her and cause great suffering. The combination of hyper-sensitivity and limited or non-existent language skills means that sudden changes from darkness to light can cause these individuals to react in extreme ways, resulting in severe pain that they are unable to express. It is also important not to use just any materials for floor or wall coverings, as they can cause significant discomfort. In short, if we are not careful, we can plunge the patient into a daily life punctuated by

---

[30] Chossy, J.-F., Boisseau, M.-T., Mattei, J.-F. (2003). La situation des personnes autistes en France: besoins et perspectives. [Retrieved February 21, 2015 from http://www.vie-publique.fr/documents-vp/chossy_ext.pdf].

multiple discomforts, suffering and other unpleasant feelings. Obviously, it is very difficult for carers to detect these disorders before they can be remedied, but it seems to us that this is one of the points on which professionals working with autistic people must focus all their attention in order to provide them with the most favourable environment.

The patient himself must also be actively considered. We absolutely must abandon the idea that autistic people do not understand what is said around them, because we now have enough evidence to affirm that this is a mistake. The consequences are indelicacy in the presence of the subject, sometimes mockery, which can be devastating for the subject's sense of confidence, already damaged by the difficulties he or she encounters on a daily basis. Physical rudeness is also often observed on the part of those caring for the most diminished patients. While it is sometimes necessary to provide physical assistance, this should be done gently and without pointing the finger at the person's disabilities. We think it's possible that autistic people have major gaps in their self-confidence, and when in doubt it's wiser to do everything as if that were the case.

Isolation is a form of abuse by renunciation that is often seen in care settings. We see patients who no one cares about any more, isolated in their rooms and left to their own devices. While it is understandable that autistic problems can cause a degree of incomprehension and frustration among carers, it is absolutely essential to maintain the patient's inclusion and interaction with them, otherwise there is a risk that they will withdraw even further into their own world.

Over-medication can also be a form of abuse, especially when it is intended to ensure the peace of mind of the staff rather than that of the patient. This phenomenon naturally exists in many facilities, to varying degrees. However, certain drugs, if administered in excessively high doses, have an influence on cognition, mood, perception of pain and many other things. It is therefore vital to watch out for signs of over-medication, so as not to add to the patient's difficulties.

If we are to take account of patients, their specific characteristics and their feelings, we need to think globally about the management of the care environment and its methods. Research is providing more and more clues about the specific features of autism, and it makes sense to use them to make patients' lives less distressing. It's a dynamic approach, based on constant observation, that can lead to better adapted care, and *de facto*, to an improvement in the subjective experience of autistic patients.

5. Conclusions

5.1. Reminder of the approach

At the end of this work, we feel it is necessary to return to the main elements that have fuelled our thinking.

First of all, we sought to define the subject of our research by defining the main characteristics of autistic pathology. Using a diachronic approach, we aimed to present and contextualise developments in autism research and clinical practice since its inception. However, we chose to free ourselves from all this work in order to adopt a neutral stance with the patients we were following. While it is true that it was difficult for us to voluntarily disregard common presuppositions and current theories in order to give direct observation every chance, we have to admit that this proved to be more than beneficial in our attempt to understand the patients.

We wanted to think of this illness as a sum of factors, which is why we addressed the question of otherness, a central issue if ever there was one, sensory disorders, which have only recently been studied, the phenomenon of regression, which fascinated us by its complexity, and the question of Asperger's syndrome, which is a verbal window on autism and thus represents a privileged means of access to it. We were thus able to bring to light contradictions and areas of misunderstanding, which we have tried to clarify in the course of our discussions.

However, some of our impressions proved to be contrary to the axioms associated with autism. And yet these are the axioms on which healthcare professionals base their work and their care. In our opinion, it would be preferable to first disregard these presuppositions in order to apprehend the patient, so to speak, 'au naturel' before embarking on any clinical work. Indeed, although the clinical phenomena we have observed with autistic children seem at first to be all similar, all equally enigmatic, with hindsight they seem to say something about the individuality of each person.

In addition, the training of professionals in contact with autism is a point that we obviously defend vigorously. It seems to us illusory to hope to approach such a complex pathology without solid theoretical tools, and it is only in this way that constructive care can be envisaged. But we would stress that the keystone seems to be, above all, real contact with the patient. The practitioner's ability to question himself and to engage in flexible personal reflection, after the event, on the phenomena he encounters will then be decisive.

Despite all the advances in research, the causes of autism are still relatively unclear. The genetic explanation, isolated in particular through the study of the prevalence of autism in twins, is intrinsically inadequate. The neurodevelopmental explanation proposes coherent models, but the operational reality is eminently more complex. Endocrinology has also made convincing progress, but is unable to explain the disparities observed within the autistic population. Since psychoanalysis was castigated, the impact of parenting has been removed from the debate on autism. Yet we and many other practitioners have noticed a certain distance between parents of autistic children. But is this a cause or a consequence? It's impossible to say. Advances in our understanding of the sensory aspects of autism open up interesting possibilities, but cannot be sufficient in themselves.

In our view, the many directions taken by research should inspire the autism clinic. If we are to understand people with this condition, we need to grasp not only what autism is from a semiological point of view, but also what it means to be autistic at a given time, in a given society. At a time when profitability and standardisation are so closely linked, the increase in the number of cases of autism raises serious questions about the future and viability of our societies. Today, the idea that autism is a way of experiencing reality is gaining ground, and it seems to us that, if not entirely correct, it is extremely fruitful in terms of the clinical openings it opens up. Rather than pathologising behaviour at all costs, it allows the observer to think about the psyche of the autistic person in a more decentred and intelligent way. This postural decentration advocated by Carl Rogers has been very useful to us in monitoring our patients.

As far as autism care is concerned, we recommend that it should be a cross-disciplinary approach. Ideally, patients should be cared for by doctors, psychologists, nurses, social workers and educators, and there should be coordinated action between these different players. In our view, it is absolutely essential to take parents into account, and no treatment worthy of the name would be possible without them. However, we do not believe that they need specific training, so that they can retain a certain spontaneity when dealing with their children. Finally, we believe it is essential to abandon, at least initially, the idea of normalising the behaviour of autistic children and adapting them at all costs to our way of life. In our view, it is more appropriate to try first of all to join them in their own world so as to apprehend them as they are, and thus lower the considerable defences they seem to put up against the outside world. Then, and only then, should we gradually readapt them to life together.

Autism is a particular reality for each patient, and needs to be considered as closely as possible to the subjective experience of the subject, abandoning "averaging" logics. This brings to mind Kanner's phrase, which we feel is all too often forgotten: *"Each case deserves, and I hope will receive, detailed consideration of its fascinating particularities"*[31].

5.2. Conclusions concerning the placement

We would like to take an analytical look at the method used at our placement, even though it is outside this field. From this point of view, we have identified a common posture of holding, in the

---

[31] Kanner, L. (1943). Autistic disturbances of affective contact. In L'autisme infantile. Introduction à la clinique relationnelle selon Kanner, (trans. G. Berquez), (p.217). Paris: PUF.

Winnicottian sense of the term. The intensiveness of the "Three I's" method lies in its non-intrusive, non-stimulating, continuous presence with the child.

This intensive, talking presence tames the child into a relationship with another person, at a time when he or she is locked in a paradox: not being able to bear separation and not being able to bear being with another person. The repetitive experience, in its dual form of physical play or play with objects, enables genuine little interactions to be introduced. They are accepted by the child because pleasure and relaxation, for both the child and the carer, are the dominant factors guiding the relationship at all times. Is it possible, in this context, to imagine a shift from the autistic object to a relational object state?

The challenge of the body seems to allow for a playful space where the other, always attentive and present, cannot be totally forgotten. It is in this space, an intermediary between the outside and the inside, that, "because there are two of us", a part of the unforeseen is played out. The child experiences, repeatedly, that his or her body is a body in relationship that can experience tuning and attachment, without this constituting an invasion by the other.

As described by D. As described by D. Anzieu in his book Du Moi-peau au moi-pensant, the primordial support for thinking comes from repeated encounters with an object that shows the child is thinking about him or herself. With the "Three I's" method, children learn to relate to others, and when they are ready to return to school, they usually spontaneously reach out to others.

But underneath the principles of the 'Three I's' method, a number of hollows emerge, which remain, and which we would like to report on in part.

5.2.1. Moving from deadly uniqueness to otherness made possible

What about the analysis of the necessary passage through a certain adhesiveness that does not obstruct the necessary separation? How can we make the right transition from two-dimensionality to three-dimensionality, from the perception of a body on the surface to that of a body incorporating a depth, a distance that allows a subject to exist in relation to an object? To be able to detach oneself, you need to have experimented sufficiently with collage, which provides structure and security. But how can we maintain the 'right distance' to avoid any risk of identity confusion?

The autistic child's fear of others legitimises the one-to-one relationship advocated by the "Three I's" method. Some of the children who have joined the Lud'Eveil Centre have previously been cared for in I.M.E.: the constant presence of the group proved unbearable for the child, and one of the immediate benefits of the method is this protection from the invasion represented by others. The results, in terms of sleep, eating, agitation and even violence, are noticeable. We can nevertheless wonder whether small activities, limited in time, with other children, might not respond to the child's curiosity, whether he or she shows it or not. Indeed, we are surprised to find that the desire for immutability of the children we met is accompanied by such an attraction for novelty. For example, familiar games in the room can sometimes arouse no interest at all, whereas all it takes is for the carer to arrive with a small bag for the child to rush off and discover its contents.

This interest in novelty is perhaps linked to a certain empathy that children show towards the person who is going to play with them: they often choose the games that we prefer, and guess what our interests are, even though we haven't talked about it. Is this empathy, is it adhesiveness? Where does a child's need for immutability end and their interest in what others are doing begin? Wouldn't time spent with small groups, alternating with frequent and sufficiently long individual time, be conducive to developing the child's buried curiosity, by introducing an element of the unexpected that is acceptable to the child?

We believe it is essential to build on this curiosity, which is present even when it is concealed, to encourage children who are alone and closed in on themselves to experience the pleasure of a relationship.

5.2.2. The place of the parent in the therapeutic relationship

In most cases, the relationships that practitioners have with parents are brief. As we have very little clinical experience, we cannot give any relevant opinion on the fact that parents are absent during play sessions with the child. There are several theories on this issue, including M. Klein, A. Freud, D. Winnicott and F. Dolto. However, it seemed to us that involving the parents directly in play sessions with the psychologist and the child could help to decompartmentalise the child and create a link between his life outside the centre, in his family, and what is happening in the centre.

Starting with play sessions with the parent, the child and the psychologist would also allow work to be done on the parent-child bond. Except when this bond is marked by too much suffering, this could provide the parent with a gradually gratifying experience of the relationship. Alternating play sessions, in threes and individually with the child, would perhaps lead to the sharing of joint attention and amazement, and then lead to pleasure and emotion.

What is at stake for the parents represents such suffering that it can give rise to ambivalent feelings, towards the child, but also towards those involved, ambivalence that we feel it is necessary to listen to and support. What's more, isn't being able to share the child's experiences from the inside, in a safe environment, a guarantee of continuity and consistency in daily life?

Supporting parents seems to us to be a particularly delicate and complex task. It is indeed the child that needs to be looked after, but the child, to use Winnicott's expression, does not exist without the parent. We cannot dissociate the child-parent couple.

In this respect, the impact of the suffering experienced by the parents requires support that is just as important as that of the child. The trauma they suffer can leave them in a state of deep distress. The dulling of their capacity to marvel at their child's small steps forward may mean that their child has expectations that he or she cannot meet.

How can we accept the child's difference, know that we have to be with him without expecting anything, as advocated by the "Three I's" method, and at the same time not expect changes or results, if possible quickly or spectacularly? What kind of back and forth, sometimes fruitless, can take place between the child and the parent, in this desire to want nothing and to want so much at the same time? Putting up with uncertainty, accompanying the child through its microvariations, with the conviction that the repetition of positive experiences will eventually become part of the psyche, is particularly trying and painful. How can we support the child and his parents without thinking, at times, that the child is resisting, or rather defending, what we silently expect of him? Are there factors that keep the child in an autistic state? How can we analyse them? How can we ensure that, in the parent-child triad, one does not move without the other?

5.2.3. Analysing stereotypies as part of an overall process

Among the many questions we ask ourselves, stereotypies are a recurring one. Stereotypes are most often perceived in a negative light, as useless and "confining".

Is it possible to read them as part of a general process corresponding to the child's development? While M.C. Laznik speaks of stereotypies as traces of unfinished work, G. Haag puts forward the hypothesis (reiterated at the CIPPA Congress in March 2015) that the very form of the stereotypy could have a link with the stage of development at which the child stopped, and that it is this stage that should be studied.

We would have liked to study the evolution of the gestures of the children we followed. If we consider that stereotypies are also a language, can we simply rejoice in their abandonment, or should we retain a certain memory of them as a specific part of the child's language, to be read in a broader context?

How can you not hear what this little autistic girl is saying as she repetitively plays with her hands?

Her gestures evolve over time: first she disarticulates her thumb, making flapping movements, then she starts to look at her hand, arm outstretched, "the eye speaks to the hand" (A. Bullinger 2010), then claps her hands waiting for someone to imitate her, demonstrating a certain authority. The gesture then changed again: she took hold of her wrists, placing them in front of her face, and sometimes stretched her mouth a little at this point.

Are these movements of coming together, of opening and closing, of sticking and unsticking, an illustration of the feeling of loss of one half of the body that has to be held together? Are they a way of integrating a space? Do they signify a search for adhesiveness, an image of the encounter, a coming together that perhaps illustrates the "noise of the encounter" referred to by Chantal Lheureux-Davidse (2003)?

It seemed to us that there was a hidden and relevant meaning in the stereotypies that needed to be grasped in order, if not to communicate with the subject, at least to enable him to feel included.

5.3 General conclusion

We would like to conclude by quoting René Roussillon: "repair never heals, in any case by itself, directly, only the empathic 'sharing of affect' relieves the solitude that characterises despair, only intelligibility makes it acceptable and relative, surmountable (...).(...) The clinical experience of autistic children shows that it is not a question of repairing or finding the object that did not come to be, but of naming what is felt in the autistic child and accompanying this feeling in empathy, so that an intelligibility of self comes about and becomes appropriable (...) To allow intelligibility in agony is to make formulable what in the object has been unusable".[32]

We are convinced that understanding the autistic child's bodily experiences, the desire to enter his world instead of taking him out of it so that he can enter ours, the deep respect for his rhythm, the putting into words of thoughts that are still unspoken, are all capable of re-establishing confidence and the possibility of existence in front of another person and, ultimately, with others. The ultimate aim of any autism clinic is to move from confining repetitive systems to repetition through imitation, so as to encourage the child's curiosity and creativity, the appropriation of his emotions and, finally, language. Now, just as there is not one autistic person but many autistic people, just as there is not one triggering factor for autism but multifactorial causes, as described by B. Gepner (2014), isn't it through a 'plural' approach, and not a 'single thought', that we can provide autistic children in such great suffering with appropriate and diversified care according to their symptoms?

At the end of our reflection, we are left with many questions. Not least of which is the unique contribution of autism. When a child emerges from autism, can we still say that the time spent on autism was wasted?

Is it not the trace of the disquieting strangeness that we all bear? Is there not a 'word' there that would enable us to escape too much normalisation? "The answer is the misfortune of the question", said M. Blanchot in *L'Entretien infini*. Only constant questioning, enriched by multidisciplinary discoveries, can maintain the research that is so impoverished when we are too focused on assertion.

If "white sounds like a space that could suddenly be understood" (Kandinsky, On the Spiritual in Art), isn't the seemingly white thought of autistic children just waiting to take shape?

Bibliography

Books and scientific journal articles

---

[32] R. Roussillon, "Agonie et désespoir dans le transfert paradoxal" in Le temps du désespoir, J. André et al Paris, PUF, 2002, p 87-88

- Asperger, H. (1944/1998). Autistic psychopaths in childhood. In Les empêcheurs de tourner en rond. Le Plessis-Robinson: Synthélabo.

- Ben-Ari, Y., Cherubini, E., Corradetti, R., Gaiarsa, J.-L. (1989). Giant synaptic potentials in immature rat CA3 hippocampal neurons. [Retrieved January 8, 2015 from http://www.ncbi.nlm.nih.gov/pmc/articles/PMC1189216/].

- Ben-Ari, Y. (2007). GABA: a primary transmitter for brain construction.
[Retrieved January 8, 2015 from http://www.medecinesciences.org/articles/medsci/full_html/2007/09/medsci2007238-9p751/medsci2007238-9p751.html#InR2].

- Bettelheim, B. (1967). The Empty Fortress. Paris: Gallimard.

- Bettelheim, B. (1975). Un lieu où renaître, Paris: Robert Laffont.

- Bergman, A., Malher, M., Pine, F. (1980). The psychological birth of the human being. Paris: Payot.

- Binet, S., Simon, T. (1907). Les enfants anormaux. Paris: Armand Colin.

- Caucal, D., Brunod, R. (2010). The sensory and motor aspects of autism. Grasse: AFD.

- Cherry, E.C. (1953). Some experiments on the recognition of speech with one and two ears, Journal of the Acoustical Society of America, 25.

- Chossy, J.-F., Boisseau, M.-T., Mattei, J.-F. (2003). La situation des personnes autistes en France: besoins et perspectives. [Retrieved February 21, 2015 from http://www.vie-publique.fr/documents- vp/chossy_ext.pdf].

- De la Presle, C., Valeton, D. (2010). Lettres à un petit prince sorti de sa bulle: une clé pour l'autisme? Paris: L'Harmattan.

- Dhossche, D. (2002). Elevated plasma gamma-aminobutyric acid (GABA) levels in autistic youngsters: stimulus for a GABA hypothesis of autism. [Retrieved January 8, 2015 from http://www.ncbi.nlm.nih.gov/pubmed/12165753].

- Frith, U. (2003). Autism: Explaining the Enigma. Oxford: Blackwell Publishing.

- Gerland, G. (2004). Une personne à part entière. Mougins: Autisme France Diffusion.

- Grandin, T. (1994). Ma vie d'autiste. Odile Jacob: Paris.

- Greenspan, S. I. (1979). Intelligence and adaptation: an integration of psychoanalytic and piagetian developmental psychology. New York: International Universities Press.

- Higashida, N. (2007). Sais-tu pourquoi je saute? (trans. D. Mitchell & D. Roche). Paris: Les arènes.

- Huriot, H. (2013). L'empereur, c'est moi. Paris: L'iconoclaste.

- Itard, J. (1801). Mémoires sur les premiers développements de Victor de l'Aveyron. Paris: Goujon.

- Itard, J. (1807). Les enfants sauvages. Paris: Seuil.

- Kanner, L. (1943). Autistic disturbances of affective contact. In L'autisme infantile, introduction à la clinique relationnelle selon Kanner (trans. G. Berquez). Paris: PUF.

- Kanner, L. (1949). Problems of nosology and psychodynamics in early childhood autism. *Am J Orthopsychiatry,* 19.
- Kanner, L. (1951). In Defense of mothers: how to bring up children in spite of the more zealous psychologists (1951). Springfield: Thomas Publisher.
- Klein, M. (1930). The importance of symbol formation in the development of the ego. In Essais de psychanalyse (pp. 263-278). Paris : Gallimard.
- Korsia-Meffre, S. (2014). Autism and related disorders: a new study reinforces the brain chlorine trail. [Retrieved January 8, 2015 from http://www.vidal.fr/actualites/13591/ autisme_et_troubles_apparentes_une_nouvelle_etude_renforce_la_piste_du_chlore_cerebral/].
- Lane, H. (1979). L'enfant sauvage de l'Aveyron. Paris: Payot.
- Leaf R. Mac Eachin, J. (2006). Autisme et ABA une pédagogie du progrès. Paris: Pearson education.
- Lévy, M. S. (undated). Autism. [Retrieved March 11, 2015 from http:// www.inventionpsychanalyse.com/autisme.php].
- Mesibov, G. (1995). Autisme: le défi du programme TEACCH. Paris: Pro Aid Autisme.
- Minkowski, E., Targowla, R. (1923). Contribution à l'étude de l'autisme : l'attitude interrogative. *L'Encéphale,* 395.
- Report by the French National Consultative Ethics Committee (2007). La situation en France des personnes, enfants et adultes, atteintes d'autisme, (102).
- Report by the French National Authority for Health. (2012). Autism and pervasive developmental disorders: coordinated educational and therapeutic interventions in children and adolescents.
- Rogers, C. (2009). Psychotherapy and human relationships: Person-centred therapy theory. Issy-les-Moulineaux: ESF Éditeur.
- Scheff, T.-J. (1966). Being mentally ill: a sociological theory. Chicago: Adline.
- Séguin, E. (1895). Rapport et mémoires sur l'éducation des enfants normaux et anormaux. Paris: Alcan.
- Tustin, F. (1990). Autisme et protection. Paris: Seuil.

Radio and television programmes:

Milton Keynes UK
Ingram Content Group UK Ltd.
UKHW011144010424
440421UK00001B/254

9 786207 300822